Law and Economics of International Telecommunications

Under the Auspices of the Max Planck Institute for Foreign and International Private Law
edited by Ernst-Joachim Mestmäcker

Volume 3

Prof. Nicolas Mateesco Matte
Dr. Ram S. Jakhu

Law of International Telecommunications in Canada

Nomos Verlagsgesellschaft
Baden-Baden

CIP-Kurztitelaufnahme der Deutschen Bibliothek

Matte, Nicolas Mateesco:
Law of International Telecommunications in Canada / Nicolas Mateesco Matte; Ram S. Jakhu. – 1. Aufl. – Baden-Baden: Nomos Verlagsgesellschaft, 1987.
(Law and Economics of International Telecommunications; Vol. 3)
ISBN 3–7890–1309–9
NE: Jakhu, Ram S.; GT

1. Auflage 1987

Editor's Preface

This book on the »Law of International Telecommunications in Canada« is part of an ongoing research project on the international communications system undertaken at the Max Planck Institute for Foreign and International Private Law in Hamburg. Like similar reports on other countries, this report is based upon questionnaires prepared at the Institute and reproduced at the end of the volume. The questionnaires are idential for all countries in order to facilitate comparative evaluations of the national reports. They serve as guidelines without, however, interfering with the authors' individual judgment in adapting their presentation to the special national situation. The project will include comparative analyses of key problem areas and the examination of the role of international organizations, the task of which is the facilitation of international communications.

The Max Planck Institute is most grateful for the cooperation of Professor Nicolas Mateesco Matte and Dr. Ram S. Jakhu. Professor Dr. Nicolas Mateesco Matte, LL.D., Q.C., O.C., R.S.C., is the Director of the Institute and Centre of Air and Space Law, McGill University, Montreal, Quebec, Canada; a member of the Barreau du Québec; a member of the Board of Directors of the International Institute of Space Law; and the past President of the International Law Association. Dr. Ram S. Jakhu, LL.M., D.C.L., is a Senior Researcher and University Lecturer in the Institute and Centre of Air and Space Law of McGill University.

We gratefully acknowledge a grant from the Volkswagen Foundation, which made this Report possible. We also extend thanks to Paul Aliferis, J.D., for his editorial assistance.

Preface

This Report forms a Canadian contribution to the project on »The Law and Economics of International Telecommunications« undertaken by the Max Planck Institute for Foreign and International Private Law in Hamburg, West Germany. The Report is divided into three parts: Part I deals with telephone services; Part II deals with remote data processing services and Part III deals with audiovisual media (TV, CATV and DBS) programs. In writing this Report, the authors followed the spirit and – whenever appropriate – the letter of the outline supplied by the Max Planck Institute. It is a general survey of the Canadian law of communications and in no way claims to be an exhaustive study of the subject.

Table of Contents

PART III: AUDIOVISUAL MEDIA PROGRAMS

LIST OF ABBREVIATIONS

A.C.	Appeal Cases
ALTA. REV. STAT.	Revised Statutes of Alberta
Atl. Prov.	Atlantic Provinces Reports
B.C. REV. STAT.	Revised Statutes of British Columbia
B.C. Stat.	Statutes of British Columbia
C.A.	Court of Appeal
CAN. CONSOL. REG.	Consolidated Regulations of Canada
CanCom	Canadian Satellite Communications, Inc.
Can. Crim. Cases	Canadian Criminal Cases
Can. Exch.	Canada Law Reports, Exchequer
Can. Pat.	Canada Patent Reports
CAN. REV. STAT.	Revised Statutes of Canada
Can. Stat.	Statutes of Canada
CAN. STAT. O. & REGS.	Statutory Orders and Regulations
Can. T.S.	Canada Treaty Series
CATV	Cable television
CCITT	International Telegraph and Telephone Consultative Committee (ITU)
C.C.L.T.	Canadian Cases on the Law of Torts
Consol. T.S.	Consolidated Treaty Series (Parry's)
CRTC	Canadian Radio-television and Telecommunications Commission
DBS	Direct broadcasting via satellite
D.L.R.	Dominion Law Reports
DOC	Department of Communications
F.C.	Federal Court Reports
F.C.T.D.	Federal Court, Trial Divison
Ga. J. Int'l & Comp. L.	Georgia Journal of International and Comparative Law
H.C.	High Court
I.L.M.	International Legal Materials
INMARSAT	International Maritime Satellite Organization
INTELSAT	International Telecommunications Satellite Organization
ITU	International Telecommunication Union
L.J.	Law Journal
L. Rev.	Law Review
L.R.Q.	Lois Refondues du Quebec
MAN. REV. STAT.	Revised Statutes of Manitoba
Man. Stat.	Statutes of Manitoba
N.B. REV. STAT.	Revised Statutes of New Brunswick
Nfld & P.E.I.	Newfoundland and Prince Edward Island Reports
NFLD. REV. STAT.	Revised Statutes of Newfoundland
N.S. REV. STAT.	Revised Statutes of Nova Scotia
OECD	Organization for Economic Cooperation and Development
Ont.	Ontario Reports
ONT. REV. STAT.	Revised Statutes of Ontario
P.C.	Privy Council
P.E.I. REV. STAT.	Revised Statutes of Prince Edward Island

PTT	Post, Telephone and Telegraph
Q.B.	Queen's Bench Law Reports
QUE. REV. STAT.	Revised Statutes of Quebec
Que. Sup. Ct.	Quebec Supreme Court
R.A.	Alberta Regulation
SASK. REV. STAT.	Revised Statutes of Saskatchewan
Sask. Stat.	Statutes of Saskatchewan
S.C.R.	Canada Law Reports, Supreme Court
SUP. CT. L. REV.	Supreme Court Law Review
TDF	Transborder Data Flow
T.I.A.S.	(U.S.) Treaties and Other International Acts
TVRO	TV Receive-Only
UCC	Universal Copyright Convention
UNIV. N.B.L.J.	University of New Brunswick Law Journal
UNTS	United National Treaty Series
U.S.T.	United States Treaties

PART I: TELEPHONE SERVICES

Chapter I: Regulation of Transborder Telephone Services

A. *Basic Regulation of Domestic Telecommunications Law for Telephone Services*

The structure and regulation of the telephone services industry in Canada is significantly different from the situation found in most other countries. Canada has no single, state-controlled umbrella organization such as the Post, Telephone and Telegraph (PTT) organizations found in many states. Instead, telecommunications services are offered by a mixture of private, governmental and joint private-governmental organizations. This has given rise to a complex mixture of federal and provincial legislation, policies and regulations. The following is a description of the Canadian telecommunications regulatory framework as it applies to telephone services and, in particular, international telephone services.

1. *Transformation of International Regulations into Domestic Law and Practice*

a) *Survey of Relevant International Law*

The international law relevant to Canadian international telephone service is derived mainly from multilateral agreements. Canada is a signatory to the ITU Convention[1] and thus adheres to its provisions on the policy and procedures for the agreement-making process that, in principle, make world-wide service operations possible. Accompanying the Convention are its Administrative Regulations, which, according to Article 42, complete the Convention and »regulate the use of telecommunication and shall be binding on all members.«

1 International Telecommunication Union (herinafter, ITU), International Telecommunication Convention (Nairobi 1982) (hereinafter, ITU Convention).

The Administrative Regulations provide a framework for the practical operation of international telecommunications services. In relation to telephone services, it is the Telegraph and Telephone Regulations[2] that provide this framework, although sections of the Radio Regulations,[3] especially concerning the use of telecommunications satellites, are pertinent. Canadian regulation of its international telephone services must be formulated in light of these Regulations.

In addition to being a party to the ITU Convention, Canada is also a party to both the INTELSAT Agreement[4] and the INMARSAT Convention,[5] while its designated telecommunications entity, Teleglobe, is the signatory to the Operating Agreements of the two organizations formed by these agreements.[6] Much of Canada's international telephone service is provided through the INTELSAT network, and thus the obligations undertaken when Canada joined this organization impact upon Canadian international telephone services regulation.

These multilateral agreements constitute the international law relevant to Canada's domestic regulation of its international telephone services. Canada is not a party to any inter-governmental bilateral agreements on the topic of telephone services, thus resulting in a paucity of pertinent international law. This arises, for the most part, from the unique style of offering telephone services in North America.

b) *Scope Reserved for National Regulation*

Much of the scope of international telephone services regulation is reserved for national regulation. First, because of the structure of the industry in Canada, international agreements can only form a general framework for Canadian regulation. The recognition of this led, in the past, to Canada's

2 ITU, Telegraph and Telephone Regulations (Geneva 1973).

3 ITU, Radio Regulations (Geneva 1982).

4 Agreement Relating to the International Telecommunications Satellite Organization »INTELSAT,« *opened for signature* Aug. 20, 1971, 23(4) U.S.T. 8313 (*entered into force* Feb. 12, 1973) (hereinafter, INTELSAT Agreement).

5 Convention on the International Maritime Satellite Organization »INMARSAT,« *opened for signature* Sept. 3, 1976, 31(1) U.S.T. 1 (*entered into force* July 16, 1979) (hereinafter, INMARSAT Convention).

6 Operating Agreement Relating to the International Telecommunications Satellite Organization »INTELSAT,« *opened for signature* Aug. 20, 1971, 23(4) U.S.T. 4091 (*entered into force* Feb. 12, 1973); Operating Agreement on the International Maritime Satellite Organization »INMARSAT,« *opened for signature* Sept. 3, 1976, 31(1) U.S.T. 135 (*entered into force* July 16, 1979).

taking reservations with regard to the Telephone Regulations to the ITU Convention adopted at Montreux in 1965: »The signature of Canada to the International Telecommunication Convention (Montreux, 1966) is subject to the reservation that Canada does not agree to be bound by the Telephone Regulations but does agree to be bound by the other Administrative Regulations except where specific reservations are made therein.«[7] After the Telegraph and Telephone Regulations had been substantially revised at a conference in April 1973, Canada was able to eliminate its reservation, and thus, with the Malaga-Torremolinos Convention,[8] there was no attached Canadian protocol. The later Regulations reduced specific details that have now become part of the CCITT[9] Recommendations, which are of a non-obligatory character.

The second reason that international telephone services regulation is reserved mainly for national regulation derives from the manner in which conventional international law is implemented by the Canadian legal system. Unlike the United States, where Senate ratification of a treaty automatically makes the treaty obligations U.S. law, Canada must follow ratification with national law to implement the obligations.[10] Thus, all regulations of international telephone services fall within the scope of national regulation, influenced by Canada's international obligations in the area.

Third, it must be noted that the Canadian regulation of its international telephone services is actually a by-product of its regulation of national telephone services. The regulatory framework for telephone services is designed primarily to meet Canadian needs and policies. International services are regulated as a part of the whole structure of telephone services. The scope of national regulation encompasses international services, implementing international law as a framework in order to enhance national services.

c) *Domestic Regulatory Power to Transform International Regulations into Domestic Law and Practice*

International law is implemented in Canada through two mechanisms. Customary international law is adopted automatically into law and applied

7 ITU, Final Protocol No. XVI for Canada to the ITU Convention (Montreux 1965).

8 ITU, International Telecommunication Convention (Malaga-Torremolinos 1973).

9 The International Telegraph and Telephone Consultative Committee (*le Comité consultatif international télégraphique et téléphonique*) studies and issues recommendations on technical, operating and tariff questions relating to telecommunications, other that those pertaining to radiocommunication.

10 This principle is stated in Attorney-General for Canada v. Attorney-General for Ontario (the *Labour Conventions* case), 1937 A.C. 326 (P.C.).

directly, unless it conflicts with a statute or some constitutional principle, in which case enabling legislation is needed.[11] Conventional international law, on the other hand, can only become law if implementing legislation is passed.[12] Canada's main obligations with respect to international telephone services are derived from conventions, and consequently the power to implement international law in the area lies with the legislative bodies competent to pass enabling legislation.

The power to implement international law domestically rests solely with the federal and provincial legislative bodies. The power to legislate is vested by the Constitution Act, 1867,[13] where jurisdiction is divided by subject between the federal and provincial levels of government. It has been law in Canada since the decision in the *Labour Conventions* case[14] that no general power to pass legislation implementing a treaty lies with the federal government. Implementing legislation must be passed by the legislature competent to make law on the particular subject matter of the treaty. Sections 91 and 92 of the Constitution Act, 1867 list the subject matters over which the federal and provincial governments, respectively, have exclusive jurisdiction.

In some cases the Constitution Act, 1867 unequivocally states under which level of government jurisdiction a subject lies. This is not the case for telephony, however. There are competing legal theses for both federal and provincial regulation of telephone services, but neither level of government has, to date, chosen to seek judicial resolution of the unsettled constitutional issues. In the absence of judicial resolution, both levels of government are exercising regulatory power in this area, giving rise to de facto divided jurisdiction. The division of juridiction is dependent upon the nature of the telecommunications entity offering the telephone service; its place and terms of incorporation and the geographic extent of its services are primary factors. Thus, for international telephone regulation to be implemented in Canada, legislatures must pass legislation for their respective jurisdictions.

The power to issue regulations affecting foreign states rests with the legislatures. The above-mentioned de facto division of jurisdiction over the subject of telephone services means that both federal and provincial legislative bodies are competent to issue such regulation with respect to their own areas of

11 The relationship of customary law to domestic law was expressed in Chung Chi Cheng v. The King, 1939 A.C. 160, 167–68 (P.C.).

12 This has been confirmed by the courts as recently as Capital Cities Communication Inc. v. Canadian Radio-Television Commission, [1978] 2 S.C.R. 141, 173.

13 British North America Act of 1867, 30 & 31 Vict., ch. 3, *as amended* (currently Constitution Act, 1867).

14 1937 A.C. 326 (P.C.).

jurisdiction. Administrative agencies and the operating companies may not issue regulations affecting foreign states unless there is delegated authority from the legislative body within whose jurisdiction they lie. The effect of such regulation would only be with respect to a foreign state operating internationally to Canada.

d) *The Contents of the International Regulations as Transformed into Domestic Law*

International telephone services are an adjunct to national telephone services in Canada. Because of this, the obligations taken on by Canada with respect to international telephone services form a regulatory framework for those services and do not set out the details of operation. It is the general guidelines found in international law that are, for the most part, implemented into Canadian law.

The manner in which the implementation of the ITU Convention is achieved is set out in the Radio Act,[15] which states in section 7(1) that »[t]he Minister may make regulation ... (d) to carry out and make effective the terms of any international agreement, convention or treaty respecting telecommunications to which Canada is a party.« In this manner, the Minister has the power to set in place the telephone guidelines provided in the Telephone Regulations.

Canada's obligations arising from the INTELSAT Agreement and the INMARSAT Convention have been more specifically introduced into domestic law. In 1948 Canada created Teleglobe, a Crown-owned corporation, by an act of Parliament.[16] It has the status of an agent of the Crown (the Government of Canada), and its purposes are, among others, »to carry on the business of public communications by cable, radiotelegraph, radiotelephone or any other means of telecommunication between Canada and any other place [and] to coordinate Canada's external telecommunication services with the telecommunication services of other nations.«

When Canada became a party to the INTELSAT Agreement, Teleglobe was the designated telecommunications entity that became the signatory for Canada to the Operating Agreement. As signatory, Teleglobe was bound by the obligations found in the Operating Agreement. Teleglobe's statutory purposes, and its status as an agent of the Crown, implemented the

15 CAN. REV. STAT. ch. R-1, *as amended* (1970).

16 Teleglobe Act, CAN. REV. STAT. ch. C-11, *as amended* (1970). Teleglobe was formerly known as the Canadian Overseas Telecommunications Corporation.

INTELSAT mechanisms in domestic law. Thus, INTELSAT regulation impacts upon domestic international telephone services.[17]
It is in this manner that international telephone services regulation is implemented in Canada.

2. *Domestic Law Unaffected by International Law*

a) *Regulatory Power*

The ultimate regulatory power over telephone services in Canada lies with the federal and provincial legislatures. The source of this power is, as already stated, the Constitution Act, 1867. This Act distributes legislative jurisdiction by subject matter to the federal and provincial governments. This distribution is complete, for one of the cardinal principles of Canadian constitutional law is that all powers must be distributed.[18] As also mentioned above, the subject matter of telephony is not clearly delineated in the Constitution Act, 1867. Proponents of exclusive federal jurisdication rely upon:

(a) Section 91, which contains federal general power to make laws for peace, order and good government of Canada in all matters not given exclusively to the provinces.
(b) Section 92(10)(a), which exempts from provincial jurisdiction »... telegraphs and other Works and Undertakings connecting the Province with any other or others of the Provinces, or extending beyond the Limits of the Province.«
(c) Section 92(10)(c), which excludes from local works and undertakings subject to provincial authority those works situated in a province that are before their execution declared by Parliament to be for the general advantage of Canada or two or more provinces.

Proponents of jurisdiction for the provinces rely upon:

(a) Section 92(16), which gives the provinces power, generally, over all matters of a merely local or private nature in the province.

17 Similarly, Teleglobe is a signatory to the INMARSAT Operating Agreement, *supra* note 6.
18 Attorney-General for Ontario v. Attorney-General for Canada, 1912 A.C. 571, 583–84 (P.C.).

(b) Section 92(10), which authorizes the provinces to legislate over local works and undertakings.
(c) Section 92(13), which authorizes the provinces to legislate on matters of property and civil rights in the provinces.

These summarize the competing federal and provincial constitutional powers upon which jurisdiction over telephone services is based. The issue remains an open one in the constitutional law of Canada. No judicial decision has resolved the contentions, and the result has been a balkanization of the telephony jurisdiction in Canada.

Under the current regulatory setting evolved by the regulatory jurisdictions of telephone services, the carriers are regulated in their entire operations either federally or provincially. Federal regulation is exercised through a number of acts. The first of these is the Railway Act,[19] which permits economic or financial control over the carrier. It does this by controlling both the tolls charged for telephone services and the agreements on the interconnection of such services.

In order to implement the powers vested by the Railway Act, a federal agency has been established and charged with exercising these powers with respect to telecommunications. This body is the Canadian Radio-television and Telecommunications Commission (CRTC).[20] The CRTC is the primary regulatory body in relation to telephony within the federal jurisdiction, regulating all carriers that fall into this jurisdiction. It has the power to issue rules, orders and regulations, as well as to make decisions on telecommunications matters.[21] Under this power, it has issued the CRTC Telecommunications Rules of Procedure,[22] setting out the procedures for approval of tariffs and inter-carrier agreements where they pertain to telecommunications.

Other federal legislation that impacts upon Canadian telephone services includes the Telesat Canada Act,[23] which established a Canadian domestic communications satellite corporation.

Parallel to the federal regulatory framework are those of the provinces, which regulate those carriers that fall within their jurisdictions. Each of the provinces has legislation establishing a board with the power to regulate

19 CAN. REV. STAT. ch. R-2, *as amended* (1970).
20 Canadian Radio-television and Telecommunications Commission Act, 1974–1976 Can. Stat. ch. 49.
21 *Id.* at § 14(2).
22 1979 CAN. STAT. O. & REGS. 554.
23 CAN. REV. STAT. ch. T-4, *as amended* (1970).

telephone carriers. These acts[24] set out the powers of the boards with respect to telephony covering tariff approval,[25] licensing regulations,[26] interconnection (provincially and otherwise)[27] and in some cases even powers concerning the standards of the equipment to be employed.[28].
Operating companies, as a rule, have limited regulatory power. That which they do have comes about from delegation or from lacunae in the regulatory framework in which they exist. The form of this power is usually either contractual or found in its approved tariffs and pertains to users of the operating company's facilities. One exception to this occurs in some of the municipally owned telephone networks, as, for example, »Edmonton Telephones.« Here it is the City of Edmonton itself that regulates the carrier, much as a provincial board or the CRTC would other carriers. Thus, the network owner has full regulatory power.

b) *A Survey of the Contents of Domestic Law*

As mentioned above, federal jurisdiction over telephone services is exercised by the CRTC through powers vested by the Railway Act. The CRTC's principal jurisdiction is over tolls,[29] including: (a) the publication, filing and approval of tariffs of tolls; (b) the justness and reasonableness of tolls; (c) the power to suspend, postpone, disallow or prescribe tolls and (d) the power to order joint tariffs with connecting companies.
The other jurisdiction conferred on the CRTC includes:

(a) The power to order interconnections with another telephone company, to prescribe terms and conditions for use and to award compensation for use;[30] and

24 Ontario Telephone Act, ONT. REV. STAT. ch. 496 (1980); Loi sur la Régie des services publics, L.R.Q. ch. R-8; Manitoba Public Utilities Board Act, MAN. REV. STAT. ch. P280 (1970); Public Utilities Board Act, ALTA. REV. STAT. ch. P-37 (1980); Electric Power and Telephone Act, P.E.I. REV. STAT. ch. E3 (1974); Newfoundland Public Utilities Act, NFLD. REV. STAT. ch. 322 (1970); Nova Scotia Public Utilities Act, N.S. REV. STAT. ch. 258 (1967); Public Utilities Act, N.B. REV. STAT. ch. P-27 (1973); Public Utilities Act, B.C. REV. STAT. ch. 325 (1960); Public Utilities Review Commission Act, 1982–1983 Sask. Stat. ch. P-45.
25 *See, e.g.*, Ontario Telephone Act, ONT. REV. STAT., ch. 457, § 26 (1980).
26 *See, e.g.*, Public Utilities Board Act, ALTA. REV. STAT. ch. P-37, § 90.1 (1980).
27 *See, e.g., id.* at § 100(1), (2) and (3) and Ontario Telephone Act, ONT. REV. STAT., ch. 496, § 99 (1980).
28 *See, e.g.*, Telephone Department Act, SASK. REV. STAT. ch. T-10, § 99 (1980).
29 Railway Act, CAN. REV. STAT. ch. R-2, § 320(2), *as amended* (1970).
30 *Id.* at § 320(7).

(b) The approval of all contracts, agreements and arrangements for interconnection and interchange of traffic, for the division of revenues between connecting companies, or generally in relation to the management, working and operation of interconnected systems or lines.[31]

In exercising its power, the role of the CRTC is regulative and corrective, not managerial. Its powers are used from time to time, either on complaint or on its own motion, to review the regulated carrier's actions and to take any necessary prospective corrective action.

The provincial boards, set up under the various provincial acts,[32] exercise powers over their respective carriers in a fashion similar to that of the CRTC. Of particular note are those powers concerning the interconnection of telephone systems. Some of the acts require that all interconnections have provincial board approval; thus, interprovincial or international, as well as intraprovincial, connections between networks must be approved, leading to a crossover between federal and provincial jurisdiction in this respect.[33]

Details of the other provincial regulatory powers mentioned above will be set out in the next section, where applicable to the issues there discussed.

B. *Legal Relations Between Domestic Carriers Providing Transborder Telephone Services and Domestic Users of Those Services*

1. *Use of Telephone Services*

a) *Public Networks (Common Carriers)*

In Canada, there are two national telecommunications systems, Telecom Canada[34] and CNCP Telecommunications (CNCP). Together they account for

31 *Id.* at § 320(11).

32 *See* enumerated acts, *supra* note 24.

33 Ontario Telephone Act, ONT. REV. STAT. ch. 496, § 99 makes provincial approval of interconnection mandatory, even if it is a connection involving federally regulated companies. The Alberta Public Utilities Board Act, ALTA. REV. STAT. ch. P-37, § 100(3), on the other hand, makes provincial approval optional if a federally regulated company is involved.

34 Known until September 1983 as the Trans Canada Telephone System.

over 90% of the $8-billion telecommunications market.[35] Telecom is an unincorporated association of the largest telephone carriers operating in each province plus Telesat Canada. The Telecom member-companies are:

British Columbia Telephone Co.
Alberta Government Telephones
Saskatchewan Telecommunications
Manitoba Telephone System
Bell Canada
New Brunswick Telephone Co. Ltd.
Maritime Telegraph and Telephone Co.
Island Telephone Co.
Newfoundland Telephone Co. Ltd.
Telesat Canada

All of the members of Telecom are privately owned, except for the three Prairie telephone companies, which are owned by their respective provincial governments, and Telesat Canada, which provides a domestic satellite telecommunications system and is jointly owned by the federal government and the major carriers. Telecom provides national telephone services to a majority of the general public.

The other national system, CNCP Telecommunications, is a privately owned partnership between divisions of the state railroad, Canadian National Railways, and the private Canadian Pacific Ltd. Unlike Telecom, CNCP provides telephone services only as leased circuits and not to the general public, although it currently has an application before the CRTC to extend its services into that area. In addition to the Telecom member-companies and CNCP, there are over 150 other, smaller telephone carriers in Canada.

International telephone services to and from Canada are divided into overseas and continental services. Teleglobe, owned by the federal government, provides facilities or otherwise arranges for telephone services between Canada and points overseas. The continental service to the United States is provided by means of interconnection agreements between Canadian telephone companies and their United States counterparts. Telecom Canada usually serves as an umbrella negotiator in securing such agreements and is the main provider of facilities for access to the United States.

The establishment of a public network requires application to the appropriate regulatory authority for approval of new operations. There are over ten such

35 Montgomery, *The Structure of Telecommunications Regulation and Markets: Canada*, in 4TH WORLD TELECOMMUNICATION FORUM, 1983 (PART III): LEGAL SYMPOSIUM ON INTERNATIONAL INFORMATION NETWORKS III.6.1, 6.3 (ITU ed. [no date]).

authorities in Canada, and the content of the application varies to some degree with each of them. The requirements of the federal regulatory agency, the CRTC, are fairly representative of the process through which the applicant must go. This will be described here, noting some exceptions found in the other regulatory agencies, but it should in no way be construed as diminishing the importance of these other authorities.

Applications to the CRTC are made under the CRTC Telecommunications Rules of Procedure.[36] The Rules initially define a »regulated company« as one subject to CRTC jurisdiction by virtue of the Canadian Radio-television and Telecommunications Commission Act.[37] The scope of this definition includes »a railway company[,] ... telephone companies and every company and person within the legislative authority of the Parliament of Canada having power to construct or operate a ... telephone system or line and to charge ... telephone tolls.«[38] The »power« spoken of is found in the constitutional documents of the respective companies.[39]

Applications to the CRTC for a new telephone network service are not made specifically for the establishment of the network. Instead they are made with respect to the approval of capital stock, approval of interconnection agreements and the approval of new tariff pages.[40] These applications are made in writing. Public notice of the application is then made in the required form. Those interested parties wishing to intervene may then file with the CRTC, submitting the requisite information. At this point, the Rules allow for the submission of interrogatories in the various proceedings and set out the obligations of the applicants in answering them.[41]

The hearings in telephone matters before the CRTC are formal. The proceedings resemble a court hearing, with sworn testimony by witnesses, cross-examination and concluding arguments. The applicant presents evidence concerning the sufficiency of his application, justifying tolls interconnections and showing the type of service to be provided. This is subject to cross-examination by interveners and by the CRTC's own counsel. Each of the interveners then presents its evidence, subject to cross-examination by interveners of adverse interest, the applicant or CRTC counsel. Concluding arguments are made, either orally or in writing. A decision is then rendered.

36 1979 CAN. STAT. O. & REGS. 554.

37 1974–1976 Can. Stat. ch. 49.

38 CAN. REV. STAT. ch. R–2, § 320(1).

39 Currently those telephone carriers regulated by the CRTC that are not railway companies or their subsidiaries are constituted by special acts of Parliament.

40 1979 CAN. STAT. O. & REGS. 554, § 4.

41 *Id.* at §§ 17–18 and §§ 13, 15 and 16.

The Federal Court of Appeal has appellate jurisdiction over all CRTC decisions. An appeal will lie on a question of law or jurisdiction upon leave of the court.[42] A decision is also open to Cabinet review. Section 64 of the National Transportation Act[43] allows the Governor-in-Council (the federal Ministerial Cabinet) to rescind any order, decision, rule or regulation of the CRTC on telecommunications matters. This may be done at any time, either on the Governor-in-Council's own motion or on the petition of an interested party. This power to review telecommunications decisions of the CRTC, in that it can be commenced on the petition of an interested party, can constitute a second avenue of appeal from a CRTC decision.

In general, the telephone regulatory authorities in Canada have the power to determine their own application procedures,[44] and – while they may not exactly follow those of the CRTC – they do tend to be most concerned with tariffs and interconnection as regards telephone services. Some do, however, have one major function that the CRTC does not, namely, a licensing function with respect to telecommunications network establishment. In Alberta, for example, the Public Utilities Board Act gives the Board the power to make licensing regulations, in addition to those concerning tariffs, interconnection, etc.[45] Thus, the status of the applicant as a public utility is evaluated.

In Canada, common carriers hold a monopoly over the general telephone services they provide within their respective areas of operation. The ultimate consumers of this service are those individuals and entities who access the public network under the conditions of the tariffs of the carriers. As will be examined later, common carriers also lease their public network lines to consumers wishing to set up private lines. This leased service is not given monopoly status, however.

The requirements for access and conditions for the use of public telephone networks are primarily the responsibility of the regulatory agency charged with overseeing a particular carrier's operations. The requirements are set by the carrier and then approved by the regulatory agency. In practice, therefore, it is the carrier's requirements for access and use that must be met. In the main, through, it is through the carrier's tariffs that access and use is regulated with respect to the public telephone network. The power to regulate tariffs rests with the regulatory agency responsible for the regulation of the particular carrier. The respective regulatory agencies receive their mandates to regulate

42 National Transportation Act, CAN. REV. STAT. ch. N-17, § 64(2) (1970).

43 *Id.* at § 64(1).

44 *See, e.g.*, Alberta Utilities Board Rules of Practice, R.A. 602–57.

45 ALTA. REV. STAT. ch. P-37, § 90.1 (1980).

from either the provincial or the federal legislature, which usually sets out the powers that the body can exercise with regard to tariff approval and modification.

For those carriers regulated by the federal government through the CRTC, the principles and powers as regard telephone services tariffs are found in the Railway Act.[46] Under section 320(3), a carrier is obliged to file with the CRTC the tariffs of:

> any telegraph or telephone tolls to be charged and such tariffs shall be in such form, size and style, and give such information, particulars and details as the Commission, from time to time by regulation or in any particular case, prescribes, and unless with the approval of the Commission, the company shall not charge and is not entitled to charge any telegraph or telephone toll in respect of which there is default in such filing, or which is disallowed by the Commission;
>
> In addition to this:
>
> The Commission may permit the classification of telegraph, telephone and cable messages into such classes as it deems just and reasonable, and may permit different rates to be charged for such different classes.[47]

The CRTC thus controls the rates and services to be offered, although it is the carriers themselves who initiate the proposals on the services and rates they wish to follow. While the above-stated powers pertain to the CRTC's regulatory authority, they are not unlike those of the other regulatory agencies. Most telephone carriers in Canada follow similar rate-setting principles and have opted for comparable rate structures. Local, residential and local business telephone services are offered on a flat-rate basis; rates for long-distance service vary with usage, i.e., distance, duration and time of day.

The CRTC also has the power of approval of joint tariffs set by a carrier falling within its jurisdiction and any other connecting carrier, regardless of under whose regulatory authority the other carrier falls.[48] This impacts on international telephone services, because through its approval power the CRTC exercises authority over the tariff structure of its regulated carriers in their arrangements with United States common carriers concerning the carriage of Canada-United States traffic. Further to this, the CRTC has the power of approval over all contracts, agreements and arrangements between a regulated carrier and any other carrier concerning division of tolls and the operation of their respective telephone services.[49]

46 CAN. REV. STAT. ch. R–2, *as amended* (1970).
47 *Id.* at § 320(4).
48 *Id.* at § 320(10).
49 *Id.* at § 320(11).

The tariff principles are set out in law in broad terms, keeping in mind the monopolistic position of the public network carriers. The basic principles that guide the CRTC in its regulatory function with respect to tariffs are that tariffs should be just, reasonable and non-discriminatory.[50] It has the power to look into all toll questions that relate to the violation of these principles and the power to substitute or prescribe satisfactory tolls to replace those that it finds wanting.[51] It should be noted again that the CRTC views its role as regulatory and corrective and does not, as a general rule, interfere with the management of its regulated carriers. It responds to complaints concerning the results of carriers' management decisions with respect to tariff rates.

The liability of a public network carrier for malfunctions of its systems is, for the most part, determined by the tort or delict law of the particular province where the damage has occurred. For those common carriers under federal jurisdiction, the Railway Act specifically forbids all means of limiting liability without the authorization of the CRTC[52] and gives the CRTC the power to make regulations to determine the extent to which a carrier's liability may be limited.[53]

In some cases the liability of the owner is more specifically laid down in legislation. In Manitoba, for example, »[a]n owner is responsible for all unnecessary damage that he wilfully or negligently causes in carrying out, maintaining, or operating any of his works.«[54] Manitoba further spells out the liability by making void any attempt by a carrier to eliminate or limit by contract the above-mentioned condition of liability.[55] In general then, carriers will be held liable for the foreseeable damage caused through negligence or willful misconduct as it pertains to the proper operation of the public network.

The power to regulate technical standards rests initially with the various legislatures. This power is not exercised to its fullest extent, since specific, prescribed technical standards are not issued under Canadian law or regulation. To a large extent, the technical standards in the Canadian telephone industry are self-developed and -administered. Canadian telecommunications technology is among the most advanced in the world, and innovations and improvements in the system are constantly being implemented by various carriers. This is supported by the government.

50 *Id.* at § 321.
51 *Id.* at § 320(5).
52 *Id.* at § 322(1).
53 *Id.* at § 322(2).
54 Public Utilities Board Act, MAN. REV. STAT. ch. P280, § 83(2) (1970).
55 *Id.* at § 90(3).

The existing legislation affecting technical standards particularly concerns the connection of network equipment and is designed to protect and enhance the quality of the technology. The CRTC's powers with respect to standards of apparatus are that:

> [u]pon any such application the Commission shall, in addition to any other consideration affecting the case, take into consideration the standards, as to efficiency and otherwise, of the apparatus and appliances of such telephone systems or lines, and shall only grant the leave applied for in case and in so far as, in view of such standards, the use, connection or communication applied for can, in the opinion of the Commission, be made or exercised satisfactorily and without undue or unreasonable injury to or interference with the telephone business of the company, and where in all the circumstances it seems just and reasonable to grant the same.[56]

The regulations of interconnection of terminal equipment by a user was until recently left to the carrier; the CRTC may now intervene to allow attachment upon satisfying itself that the standards of the connecting equipment are not harmful to the operation of the carrier. The CRTC thus has control to assure that substandard equipment is not used and also that carriers do not impede innovation. Further detail as to the CRTC liberalization of its policy on user-provided equipment attachment is found later in this chapter (Section B, 2).

Government support for high technology vis-à-vis Canadian telephone services is also seen in the international telecommunications duties of the Minister of Communications. The Department of Communications Act[57] states that the Minister, in exercising his functions, shall »take such action as may be necessary to secure, by international regulation or otherwise, the rights of Canada in communication matters.«[58] One way in which the Minister exercises this duty is through Canada's participation in the CCITT, which as stated in a DOC publication »provides the means of ensuring to the greatest extent possible that the recommendations of the CCITT are compatible with the technical characteristics of the Canadian telecommunications network and Canadian operating practises. Incompatibilities in this regard can result in heavy cost penalties to Canadian subscribers and the operating organizations

56 Railway Act, CAN. REV. STAT. ch. R–2, *as amended* (1970).
57 CAN. REV. STAT. ch. C-24, *as amended* (1970).
58 *Id.* at § 5(1)(f).
59 DEPARTMENT OF COMMUNICATIONS TELECOMMISSION, INTERNATIONAL IMPLICATIONS OF TELECOMMUNICATIONS: THE ROLE OF CANADA IN INTELSAT AND OTHER RELEVANT INTERNATIONAL ORGANIZATIONS (Study 3(a) 1971).

involved.«[59] Canada strives to maintain standards both compatible with international networks and of high quality.
The regulatory decision process, discussed in this section, is open to review by the courts. As previously mentioned, the Federal Court of Appeal has appellate jurisdiction over the decisions of the CRTC.[60] In addition, a second avenue of appeal is possible through section 64 of the National Transportation Act, which gives the Governor-in-Council power to review telecommunications decisions of the CRTC upon the petition of an interested party.
As regards appeals from decisions of the various provincial regulatory agencies, the procedure is usually laid out in the agency's constituent legislation. Appeals from decisions of these agencies are usually to the courts of the respective provinces.[61] In some cases, the provincial cabinet also has the power to review these decisions, much as the Governor-in-Council may review CRTC decisions.[62]

b) *Private Networks*

In Canada, a private network refers to circuits from common carriers by customers for their private use. Leased circuits are readily available in most regions on a competitive basis from telephone carriers and CNCP Telecommunications. The monopoly situation found in public network services does not apply. Because there is a more competitive basis for this service, the regulatory framework that governs it is not as pervasive.
The terms and conditions regulating the provision and use of leased circuits are normally incorporated either in a contract between the carrier and the user or in a carrier's tariffs. Such conditions usually require the approval of the appropriate regulatory agency, subject to governing legislation. Carriers under federal jurisdiction operate under the authority of CRTC, which »may by regulation prescribe the terms and conditions under which any traffic may be carried by the company.«[63]
The establishment and operation of a private network requires no particular application to regulatory authorities. Rates for leased circuits, while subject to regulatory approval, have largely been determined by competition, and, as a

60 National Transportation Act, CAN. REV. STAT. ch N-17, § 64(1) (1970).
61 *See, e.g.*, Ontario Telephone Act, ONT. REV. STAT. ch. 496, § 19(1) (1980), which provides for an appeal to the Divisional Court.
62 *Id.* at § 18 gives the Ontario Cabinet various powers to review decisions of the Board.
63 Railway Act, CAN. REV. STAT. ch. R-2, § 322(3), *as amended* (1970).

result, telephone-carrier and CNCP tolls for leased circuits are comparable. Customers may choose between the public network and leased facilities in accordance with their own needs.
The sublease, for purposes of either sharing or resale, of leased circuits is generally not permitted. Canadian law does not specifically allow or forbid subleasing of private lines; it is left to the appropriate regulatory agency to make the decision when they approve the lease agreement as to whether conditions of sublease would be appropriate. Currently no subleasing occurs in Canada, since common carriers do not permit such in the conditions of their leases and the regulatory agencies have accepted these conditions.
As regards the provision of international leased circuits, Teleglobe is responsible for overseeing this area. In providing these circuits, the relevant recommendations of the CCITT are applied.[64]

2. *Admission of Terminal Equipment to the Network*

The issue of the admission to the carrier's network of terminal equipment other than that owned by the carrier has been an important one in the recent development of telephone services in Canada, which has moved from a position of little or no extra equipment to a much freer situation in just a few years. Under domestic law, all terminal equipment of whatever type that is connected to a carrier's network is considered to be part of the network and is regulated by the appropriate authority. This may be stated specifically in such legislation as is found in Nova Scotia[65] or in Manitoba, where »terminal attachment« is defined as »any equipment device or contrivance capable of transmitting, routing or receiving messages or signals through the telephone services offered by the Commission through the system, but does not include a passive telephone answering device.«[66] On the other hand, this may be implied from the jurisdiction and scope of the regulatory authority given to the board. The CRTC has this set out in section 320(9) of the Railway Act in this manner.

64 CCITT, GENERAL TARIFF PRINCIPLES – CHARGING AND ACCOUNTING IN INTERNATIONAL TELECOMMUNICATIONS SERVICES: RECOMMENDATIONS OF THE D SERIES (CCITT »Red Book« vol. II.1) (1985).
65 Nova Scotia Public Utilities Act, N.S. REV. STAT. ch. 258, § 1(g) (1967).
66 An Act to Amend the Manitoba Telephone Act, 1982–1984 Man. Stat. ch. 66.

The regulation of the admission of terminal equipment to a network was, until recently, left to the network owner. Ultimate regulatory authority lay with the federal and provincial legislations, which, for the most part, delegated that authority to the various regulatory boards. These, in turn, upheld the attachment regulations found in the tariffs of the various public network carriers. This meant that only limited types of equipment not owned by the carrier were able to be attached.

The rationale behind allowing these protective measures was that they protected the network as well as its development and maintained lower charges for basic telephone services. The exclusion of customer-provided equipment by carrier tariffs was not total; they provided for exemptions in certain specified cases. Exemptions could be made by agreement with the carrier or prescribed in the tariffs (usually passive devices or those that did not address the network system).

This restrictive attitude began to ease in the late 1970s, due to pressure from terminal manufacturers and users seeking a freer market. The first significant change occurred in the federal area of jurisdiction with the CRTC's Telecom Decision 80-13, which prescribed »Interim Requirements Regarding the Adjustment of Subscriber-Provided Terminal Equipment.« This decision modified Bell Canada's tariffs to allow customer-provided telephones to be attached to the carrier's facilities. Public hearings on the issue were then held by the CRTC in 1981, and in November 1982 it released a major decision.[67] Liberalization of attachment regulations was not only to be continued but was to be extended beyond Bell Canada's tariffs to other carriers under its jurisdiction, thus encompassing services provided to 70% of the Canadian market.

The decision provided that all equipment manufactured after September 1, 1983 be certified as meeting the technical requirements established by the Department of Communications Terminal Attachment Program if it is to be attached to the public switched telephone network.

With this decision began a national trend toward liberalizing terminal-attachment regulations. Various provinces introduced legislation allowing the attachment of user-provided equipment, subject to compliance with certain basic technical criteria intended to protect public networks. Even those provinces where the major carrier is provincially owned introduced more liberal attachment policies. Manitoba, for example, while ruling that no person other than carrier could in principle connect to the system any terminal attachment, allowed exceptions for those attachments authorized under

67 CRTC Telecom. Dec. 82–14.

regulation for the purposes of residential extension telephone sets or a terminal attachment authorized by an agreement between the carrier and the person making the attachment.[68] These terms are more restrictive than those found in the CRTC decision, yet they are more liberal than an attachment prohibition.

As with other decisions of regulatory agencies in Canada, those concerning equipment attachment are subject to review on questions of law or jurisdiction by a superior court. The actual court varies from province to province. Furthermore, cabinet review is also usually available.

C. *Legal Relations between Domestic and International or Foreign Network Operators*

International connection between domestic telephone services and the international network is divided into continental and overseas services. Connections to points in the United States have long been provided through arrangements between Canadian carriers and their United States counterparts. Overseas connections, on the other hand, are established through Teleglobe and its association with INTELSAT and INMARSAT, as well as through its cable lines. Domestic carriers make the outward link through agreements with Teleglobe.

1. *Requirements of Domestic Telecommunications Law for Access to the International Network*

In Canada access to the international network (»gates«) for telephone services is through United States carriers or Teleglobe. The requirements for gating to the international network are found, for the most part, in domestic law. International law, however, does impact on these requirements when the gating is through Teleglobe.

The statutory role of Teleglobe is, inter alia, to carry out Canada's obligations with respect to INTELSAT. As such it is the mechanism by which domestic law implements the international obligations that follow from the INTELSAT Agreement. INTELSAT sets a number of standards that impact upon

68 *Id.*

domestic linkage to its network. For instance, it determines the rates for the utilization of the INTELSAT space segment.[69] Teleglobe thus determines its rates using INTELSAT rates as a basis. Furthermore, INTELSAT sets technical standards to ensure compatibility with its space segment, and this power includes approval of earth stations for access to the INTELSAT space segment.[70] Consequently, Teleglobe must ensure that any domestic network gating into the INTELSAT network meets the technical standards.

The terms for gating are set down in the contract between Teleglobe and the domestic network. This means that conditions are established by Teleglobe, which is, in effect, self-regulatory in this respect: Teleglobe, in its telephone operations, is not regulated by any regulatory body, such as the CRTC, and thus is left to make agreements on its own. As an agent of the Crown, however, it is subject to governmental power and must follow policy directives from the Crown. The particulars of Teleglobe contracts with domestic networks and international cable consortia are not generally available publicly.

The requirements for gating through United States carrier networks are fundamentally products of domestic law. Such interconnection is achieved by separate private agreements between Canadian and United States carriers, subject to approval by the appropriate regulatory agency. For those Canadian carriers under federal jurisdiction, this approval authority rests with the CRTC.[71] The terms and conditions found in the agreements are, however, determined by the contracting parties.

One such agreement is that between Telecom (often the representative of the domestic networks) and AT&T, signed in 1971. This agreement sets out the general principles for establishing an interconnection between the two networks. It sets up a »clearing house« to effect payments and partition the revenues flowing from the connection (article 9(a)). Article 4 of the agreement states that the services offered will be non-discriminatory and follow a first-come, first-serviced handling policy. Article 5 declares that rates will be approximately the same in both directions. In addition, article 13 reiterates that all terms and conditions of the agreement are subject to all necessary governmental licenses and approvals.

From the above, it can be seen that the regulatory power over the legal relations between domestic and international networks is primarily exercised by the operating companies through private contracts. The power ultimately

69 INTELSAT Agreement, *supra* note 4, at art. VIII(b.)(v)(C).
70 *Id.* at art. VIII(b.)(v)(A).
71 Railway Act, CAN. REV. STAT. ch. R–2, § 320(1).

rests with the domestic legislatures, which, through their regulatory agencies, have the power of approval over all such agreements. Regulatory power is also exercised to some extent by international organizations, such as INTELSAT. In the final analysis, though, it is the operating carriers themselves that determine the everyday legal structure of the relationship.

2. *Requirements of Domestic Telecommunications Law for the Use of the International Network*

The fundamental domestic requirement for a carrier with regard to interconnection with the international network is that the appropriate regulatory agency approve the interconnection. Such approval is similar to that which must be acquired for domestic interconnection because it is derived from the same source. The regulatory agency has the authority to approve the connection itself, the international tariff rates, the accounting procedures, etc., of the carrier with respect to the international link. The CRTC, for example, has such power over the telephone carriers under its jurisdiction as is vested by the Railway Act,[72] which makes no differentiation as to the type of interconnection – domestic or international – that a carrier makes.

The regulatory setting for tariffs and technical standards was described in the previous section and will be only summarized here. Ultimate regulatory powers lie with the federal and provincial legislatures and their delegated regulatory bodies, with regulatory input from international organizations in some cases. The operating companies, however, are the practical determiners of the rates and technical standards, and this occurs to a far greater extent in the continental international arena because the agreements are worked out between private entities, as in the above-mentioned case between Telecom and AT&T.

72 *Id.* at §§ 320, 321.

Chapter II: Legal Regulation of the Terminal and Network Equipment Markets

A. *Demand Side*

1. *The Impact of the Regulation of Telephone Services on the Terminal and Network Equipment Markets*

a) *Procurement of Equipment*

Telephone equipment is procured in Canada by two main groups: network owners/operators and network users. The freedom of choice that they enjoy with regard to this procurement is not equal. Domestic telecommunications rules allow network owners/operators a relatively broad freedom of choice. They are subject to their respective regulatory bodies, to which, to a greater or lesser extent, has been delegated the authority to approve equipment standards of equipment. In this way the regulatory body can assure – especially when interconnection occurs – that physical or economic harm does not result for any of the parties.

The power given to the CRTC is set forth in section 320(9) of the Railway Act. The criteria laid down here, however, are only with respect to the »standards, as to efficiency and otherwise.« This does not empower the CRTC to reject equipment because it is of foreign manufacture or for any other similar reason. Canadian network operators and owners are thus not restricted in the source of their equipment. Although domestic production of telecommunications equipment is protected to some degree by relatively high tariffs, Canadian manufacturing companies develop and manufacture some of the most advanced telecommunications equipment in the world. These factors lead to much of the network equipment being procured in Canada. This also means that Canadian network owners/operators are in a good competitive position when it comes to the purchase of equipment and are able to choose the best and most electronically and economically efficient material that is available.

Network users, on the other hand, are rather restricted in their choice of equipment. Until recently, user-provided terminal attachment was not generally permitted. Telephone carriers often restricted such attachment, ostensibly to protect their networks and maintain lower charges for basic telephone service; only the carrier itself could provide terminal equipment, and restrictive tariffs were permitted by the regulatory agencies. The attachment of nonaddressing equipment, such as computer terminals and answering machines, was an exception to the general nonattachment policy.

Concerns, however, arose over the validity of the carriers' assertions about system protection, and a move towards liberalization began. For users whose carrier is under federal jurisdiction, there is now considerable choice. The CRTC, in a major 1982 decision,[73] concluded that liberalization of its terminal attachment policy would be a good thing. Under this decision, all equipment manufactured after September 1, 1983 – and meeting technical standards established by the DOC Terminal Attachment Program – can be attached to public switched telephone networks. The technical standards for terminal equipment are developed by the Terminal Attachment Program Advisory Committee (TAPAC). To be certified, all equipment, regardless of origin, must be tested by a DOC-approved laboratory. Standards are published for both network-nonaddressing and network-addressing devices.

This liberalization has allowed a wide variety of equipment to become available to the network users of carriers under CRTC jurisdiction. It has also led other regulatory agencies to a more liberal approach to equipment attachment, although usually not to the same extent as that of the CRTC.

b) *The Conditions for the Procurement of Equipment*

The power to set the conditions for procuring telephone equipment belongs to the federal and provincial legislatures. To a great extent, this power has been delegated to the various regulatory bodies charged with overseeing the telephone networks.[74] This power to set standards is established in the constituent legislation of such agencies.[75] Since this power has not been exercised to its full extent, carriers generally have had a relatively free choice when procuring network equipment. The major exercise of standard-setting power has been to affirm carrier tariffs that restrict the attachment of user-provided equipment. Because of the manner in which regulatory agencies

73 Telecom. Dec., *supra* note 67.

74 Until recently, Saskatchewan had no regulatory board. However, with the entry into force of the Public Utilities Review Commission Act, 1982–1983 Sask. Stat. ch. P–45.1, all provinces now have such a board.

75 *See* enumerated acts, *supra* note 24.

have used their authority, the conditions for equipment procurement have been, for all practical purposes, set by network owners/operators. Although this is still true of network equipment procurement, the situation is changing for user-provided equipment with the liberalization of terminal-attachment policies.

Telecommunications regulatory agencies, in particular, the CRTC, have taken a more active role in exercising their authority with respect to equipment procurement. As mentioned in the previous section, the CRTC has amended the tariffs of those carriers that fall under its jurisdiction, allowing user-provided terminal equipment with the proper DOC certification to be attached to such networks. In making this decision, the CRTC is reacquiring some of the delegated power to set conditions for equipment – a power that rested with it from the beginning.

One other influence on the power to set conditions for equipment procurement is the international regulatory framework provided by Canada's treaty obligations. The use, for international telephone service, of the Teleglobe/INTELSAT gate introduces INTELSAT standards into the procurement of equipment that accesses this gate. INTELSAT sets standards for the earth stations that access its space segment. Teleglobe, in turn, must ensure that equipment connected to its system by domestic carriers is compatible. This effectively gives INTELSAT the power to set conditions for the type of network equipment to be procured.

The conditions for procurement of network equipment by Canadian telephone carriers are largely determined by the forces of the marketplace. However, domestic production of telecommunications equipment has been protected to some extent by relatively high most-favoured-nation tariffs. These are in place to help counter the fact that many countries have government-owned telephone carriers, whose procurement policies foster their domestic industry.[76] Competition remains keen, however, among the world's manufacturers, and the recent liberalization of equipment policies in Canada has enhanced this, especially in the category of transmission products.[77] Also, carriers know the value in continued use of the most advanced equipment and will seek to maintain high standards, sometimes at greater cost. Government policy encourages high standards, both nationally and internationally.[78]

76 RESTRICTIVE TRADE PRACTICES COMMISSION, MINISTER OF SUPPLY AND SERVICES, TELECOMMUNICATIONS IN CANADA: PHASE III – THE IMPACT OF VERTICAL INTEGRATION ON THE EQUIPMENT INDUSTRY (1983).

77 *Id.* at 69.

78 The Department of Communications Act, CAN. REV. STAT. ch. C–24, § 5(1), *as amended* (1970), mandates that »[t]he Minister of Communications ... shall ... (b) promote the

With respect to terminal equipment, the conditions for procurement are more regulated. The network owners/operators have the same type of choice that they have for network equipment and are largely self-regulated. For user-provided equipment, however, regulation has recently developed, at least at the level of federal jurisdiction. The CRTC decision[79] liberalizing attachment furnishes users a choice in the connection of all certified terminal equipment. Single-line residential subscribers may now own all their telephones, including the main set. Single-line and business subscribers are able to choose whether to own or lease their telephones, as are multiline business customers.
The certification of terminal equipment (and this means all equipment, regardless of place of origin) is carried out by the DOC or DOC-accredited laboratories. Technical standards are developed by the Terminal Attachment Program Advisory Committee, a DOC-chaired organization that includes voluntary participants from among carriers, manufacturers, suppliers, users and provincial governments. The standards are published under the Terminal Attachment Program.[80]
The free attachment of user-provided equipment raises questions concerning equipment maintenance. Before liberalization, the carrier maintained most terminal equipment. Now, at least in the case of Bell Canada, the company has left the full maintenance burden to the equipment owner. This has been approved by the regulatory agency and would seem to be the logical norm following liberalization.

2. *The Impact of Other Regulations on the Terminal and Network Equipment Markets*

The Combines Investigation Act[81] has had a considerable impact on the regulation of the terminal equipment market in Canada. The current liberalization of the user-provided attachment policy resulted directly from an investigation into the telecommunications equipment industry that was initiat-

establishment, development and efficiency of communications systems and facilities for Canada ... [and] (f) take such action as may be necessary to secure, by international regulation or otherwise, the rights of Canada in communication matters.«

79 Telecom. Dec., *supra* note 67.

80 The inclusion of the standards is beyond the scope of this work. For details see Department of Communications publications CP-01 and CS-01, 02, 03, 04 and 05.

81 CAN. REV. STAT. ch. C–23 (1970).

ed under the Act. This led directly to an inquiry by the Restrictive Trade Practices Commission under section 47 of the Act.

The report[82] from the inquiry set out several recommendations as to what should occur in the industry. Among these are:

a) Customer ownership of terminals and an increased number of suppliers would be a growing source of increased efficiency and must be accommodated.

b) Unregulated sale and rental markets should be permitted to develop in terminal equipment.

c) Although interconnection would result in increased sales of foreign-made equipment in Canada, the Canadian industry has reached a sufficiently high level of strength and maturity, such that it is not premature to expect fair competition in the Canadian market. Steps must be taken, however, to ensure that markets closed to imports through non-tariff barriers are made accessible to Canadian manufacturers in accordance with the spirit and the letter of GATT.

d) Standards for all terminal equipment should be established through the Terminal Attachment Program, and a deadline should be set by the government for the completion of this task. CTRC should have the authority to review standards should parties to the certification program establish to its satisfaction that the standards were unnecessarily restrictive and would eliminate certain equipment from the market.[83]

Much of this has been put in place, and it may thus be seen that the inquiry initiated under the regulatory authority of the Combines Investigation Act has played an important part in the development of the regulatory regime of the terminal equipment market.

B. *Supply Side: The Effect of the Demand-Side Situation on the Access of Suppliers to the Market for Network and Terminal Equipment*

The network equipment market, being generally an industry-regulated one, is responsive to its demand-side situation and is a product of it. As already

82 RESTRICTIVE TRADE PRACTICES COMMISSION, MINISTER OF SUPPLY AND SERVICES, TELECOMMUNICATIONS IN CANADA: PHASE I – INTERCONNECTION (1979).

83 *Id.* at 202–03.

pointed out, carriers are able to choose their equipment freely; thus, demand dictates the market, with some influence from protective tariffs.[84]

The effect of the demand-side situation on the terminal equipment market has evolved differently. Because user-provided equipment was restricted by the carriers' tariffs, the demand side played a lesser role in determining the market than it would otherwise have. Demand was created only by the carriers; user input was minimal. Users, however, found this situation unsatisfactory, not so much from a technical standpoint but from one of economy: user-provided equipment could save the user money. Demand-side pressures increased, and the traditional network-protection arguments against user-provided terminals were challenged. The effect has been the liberalization of the terminal-attachment policies. This has opened up the terminal equipment market, which is now, except for equipment certification standards, a freer market.

84 *See supra* pp. 39–40.

PART II: REMOTE DATA PROCESSING

Chapter III: Legal Regulation of Transborder Data Flow

A. *Introduction*

For the purposes of this study, the term transborder data flow (TDF) will be limited to the concept of computer-to-computer transmission and excludes such information transfer as voice telephony and broadcasting. The limited regulation that pertains to transborder flow in these areas is covered in Part I and Part III, respectively. As such, TDF arises when data, as digitally encircled, computer-readable bits of information, is transformed, stored or processed in more than one nation.[85]

The legal regulation of TDF in Canada is in its infancy. There is currently little regulation of any kind that applies to the control of TDF. This paucity of regulation does not, however, accurately reflect Canada's interests and concerns over TDF. As one author has recently stated:

> Canada is one of the first countries to make a comprehensive examination of the possible effects of TDF and the information revolution. Canada is also one of the few countries that have [sic] attempted to calculate the economic costs, such as opportunity loss, job loss, reduction in job creation, and the eventual effect on balance of payments. All studies on TDF sponsored by the Canadian Government contain a disclaimer denying any direct relationship between the study and government policy.[86]

As far back as 1971, the Canadian government inquired into the long-term effects of the emerging information technology. A Department of Communications study, *Instant World*,[87] identified concerns with respect to computers, including the issues of privacy,[88] the protection of intellectual property,[89] interconnection and economic impact.[90]

85 *See* Novotny, *Transborder Data Flow Regulation: Technical Issues of Legal Concern*, 3 COMPUTER L.J. 105 (1982).

86 Yarn, *The Development of Canadian Law on Transborder Data Flow,* 13 GA. J. INT'L & COMP. L. 825, 826 n.5 (1983).

87 DEPARTMENT OF COMMUNICATIONS, INSTANT WORLD: A REPORT ON TELECOMMUNICATIONS IN CANADA (1971).

88 *Id.* at ch. 4.

89 *Id.* at ch. 5.

90 *Id.* at ch. 14.

Instant World was followed by a more specific inquiry on computer communications, entitled *Branching Out.*[91] It examined, in particular, the economic aspects of the issue and their impact on the Canadian economy at large. A number of negative factors with respect to TDF were identified:

a) foreign-owned corporations control the basic technology;
b) the Canadian market alone will not produce a satisfactory return on investment;
c) the dynamics and economics of U.S.-based operations with branches in Canada favour the adoption of U.S. TDF; and
d) research and development in Canada is not sufficiently capitalized to create a viable product base in hardware or software.[92]

More recently, the *Clyne Report*[93] defined the sovereignty issues related to TDF. These include such problems as the dependence on foreign data banks, the erosion of the Canadian cultural and national identity, the decreased control over domestic economic affairs and the decline in Canada's international competitive abilities. This report urged immediate regulation of TDF to ensure control over information that could be vital to Canada's sovereignty.[94] Such regulation has not yet been forthcoming.

The main reason for this absence of regulation is that the Canadian response to the identified problems associated with TDF has been deliberated and restrained. A balance must be struck between regulatory restraints and freedoms. The result of this approach hopefully will be well-targeted legislation designed to protect the Canadian industries that are particulary vulnerable to TDF[95] while, at the same time, not inhibiting the development of the technology.

The following will examine the regulatory framework now in place in Canada that impacts on TDF. The power to regulate and the limited current legislation pertaining to TDF will be discussed.

91 COMPUTER/COMMUNICATIONS TASK FORCE, BRANCHING OUT: REPORT OF THE COMPUTER/COMMUNICATIONS TASK FORCE (1972).

92 *Id.* at 76–77.

93 CONSULTATIVE COMMITTEE ON THE IMPLICATIONS OF TELECOMMUNICATIONS FOR CANADIAN SOVEREIGNTY, TELECOMMUNICATIONS AND CANADA (the Clyne Report) (1979).

94 *Id.* at recommendation 24.

95 Yarn, *supra* note 86, at 826.

B. *Regulatory Authority with Respect to TDF*

The source of regulatory power over TDF is ultimately the Constitution Act, 1867.[96] The subject matters over which the federal and provincial governments have exclusive jurisdiction are enumerated in sections 91 and 92, respectively. TDF is not specifically enumerated, and, to determine under which level of government jurisdiction lies, TDF has to be fitted into the list by analogy. Constitutional issues of this type are usually resolved judicially, but as yet there have been no court decisions on the matter.

The nature of TDF does, however, bring it within the ambit of point-to-point telecommunications (i.e., nonbroadcasting telecommunications), which, as discussed in Part I on telephony, currently has two competing legal theses as to which level of government holds jurisdiction.[97] Neither thesis has been given judicial approval, and this has resulted in a de facto situation, where both levels of government regulate aspects of point-to-point telecommunications. Consequently the de facto situation for TDF is that regulatory legislation can be created by either the federal or provincial legislatures.

Moreover, this de facto situation is also subject to a deliberate policy of maintaining the status quo. The federal government, out of deference to the political problems it might create and a sense that it would not be in the public interest, seems reluctant to seek exclusive jurisdiction over all point-to-point telecommunications. Provincial governments, on the other hand, are unwilling to risk what they have by mounting a possibly losing challenge for greater powers. Divided jurisdiction for TDF, it seems, will continue.

Even if the constitutional issue of exclusive legislative jurisdiction over point-to-point telecommunications were to be resolved in the courts, it may not follow that only the federal or provincial governments would have exclusive jurisdiction to regulate all aspects of TDF. It is the nature of TDF that it may be utilized in many industries. The regulation of various industries in Canada falls within the power of both levels of government, and thus regulations created within the ambit of either jurisdiction that impacted upon TDF could be legitimate, even should they incidentally encroach upon exclusive regulatory authority over TDF.[98] Consequently, the two levels of

96 British North America Act of 1867, 30 & 31 Vict., ch. 3, *as amended* (currently Constitution Act, 1867).

97 *See supra* p. 20.

98 Should there however be a conflict between federal legislation and provincial legislation in areas where jurisdiction overlaps, federal legislation prevails. Provincial Secretary of P.E.I. v. Egan, 1941 S.C.R. 396.

government may have regulatory authority over TDF that is ancillary to other areas of juisdiction.

C. *Domestic Regulation of TDF*

As mentioned, despite considerable government interest in the effects of the developing TDF technology and use, little has been done by way of legislative regulation. The only legislation specifically designed to create legal restrictions preventing the transborder flow of data has been in the area of banking, which falls under the jurisdiction of the federal government.[99] This – along with the federal regulatory power in point-to-point telecommunications – gives Parliament the authority to regulate TDF. The measure taken was introduced into law in the Bank and Banking Law Revision, 1980[100] and is directed at alleviating some of the concerns over sovereignty erosion that arose from increased TDF. The Act states that a bank shall maintain in Canada:

> (a) a record showing, for each customer of the bank on a daily basis, particulars of the transactions between the bank and that customer and the balance owing to or by the bank in respect of that customer, and
> (b) all registers and other records referred to in subsection (1), and *shall maintain and process in Canada any information or data* relating to the preparation and maintenance of such records.[101]

Furthermore:

> Where a bank, in accordance with subsection (5), maintains copies or extracts of any records or registers referred to in subsection (4) or further processes information or data relating to such copies or extracts outside Canada, the bank shall so inform the Inspector and provide him with a description of the nature of those copies or extracts maintained outside Canada and a description of the further processing of information or data relating to such copies or extracts outside Canada and such other information as the Inspector may require from time to time; and in the event that the Inspector is at any time of the opinion that the further processing outside Canada of information or data relating to any such copies or extracts is incompatible with the fulfilment [sic] of his responsiblities under this Act or he is advised by the Minister [of Finance] that, in the opinion of the Minister, such

99 British North America Act of 1867, 30 & 31 Vict., ch. 3, § 91, *as amended* (currently Constitution Act, 1867).
100 1980–1983 Can. Stat. ch. 40.
101 *Id.* at § 157(4) (emphasis added).

further processing is not in the national interest, he shall direct the bank to further process information or data relating to such copies or extracts in Canada and the bank shall forthwith comply with any such direction.[102]

Thus, the primary processing of data must be conducted in Canada, and the Inspector of Banks may suspend extraterritorial data processing of bank records if it is consistent with his duty to maintain the integrity of the Canadian banking system. The Minister of Finance also has the power to advise the Inspector of Banks to suspend all data processing by banks outside Canada if the Minister concludes it is in the national interest. This latter power is a strong implement for exercising policy decisions with regard to informatics.[103]

The amendments to the Bank Act[104] indicate the regulatory actions of the federal government vis-à-vis economic and sovereignty concerns over TDF. Concerns about privacy, though less intense, have resulted in legislative action. The Canadian Human Rights Act[105] and the later Access to Information and Privacy Act[106] address the issue of a Canadian citizen's access and control rights over his personal data. The provisions, while giving access to personal data and the right to correct erroneous data, are applicable only to government data banks.[107] These Acts, however, created the office of Privacy Commissioner,[108] which, besides being a »watch dog« regarding the government-related provisions, has been charged with:

[carrying] out or caus[ing] to be carried out such studies as may be referred to the Commissioner by the Minister of Justice
(a) relating to the privacy of individuals,
(b) concerning the extension of the rights to which individuals are entitled under this Act in respect of personal information about themselves, and
(c) relating to the collection, retention, disposal, use or disclosure of personal information by persons or bodies, other than government institutions, that come within the legislative authority of Parliament,

102 *Id.* at § 157(6).

103 Informatics has been defined as »the rational and systematic application of information to economic, social and political development.« INFORMATICS: ITS POLITICAL IMPACT, I.B.I. Doc. DGI–04, at 2 (1980); *reprinted in* Yarn, *supra* note 86, at 832 n. 32.

104 CAN. REV. STAT. ch. B–1 (1970), *repealed by* Bank and Banking Law Revision, 1980, 1980–1983 Can. Stat. ch. 40.

105 1976–1977 Can. Stat. ch. 33.

106 1980–1983 Can. Stat. ch. 111.

107 1976–1977 Can. Stat. ch. 33, § 50(1).

108 Initially created by the Canadian Human Rights Act, *see id.* at §§ 57–61, the post was reestablished with the Access to Information and Privacy Act, 1980–1983 Can. Stat. ch. 111, §§ 53–67 (schedule II).

and the Privacy Commissioner shall report thereon to the Minister of Justice from time to time.[109]

A regulatory mechanism is thus in place at the federal level to expand the current provisions of these Acts to cover the private sector, with attendant ramifications for the regulation of TDF.
As mentioned, Parliament is not the only authority that may issue laws that affect TDF; provincial legislatures have this power, both as ancillary to their recognized legislative jurisdiction and as de facto in the field of point-to-point telecommunications (though limited to non-radiowave telecommunications). As with the federal counterpart, this power is seldom exercised. Perhaps the only provincial law to impact directly on TDF (although not directly designed to do so) is the Business Records Protection Act[110] of Ontario, which prohibits the production of any document requested by a foreign tribunal, unless such a document is normally sent out of the province in the regular course of business.[111] The Act is designed to counter United States attempts at extending its extraterritorial antitrust jurisdiction. In effect it creates a ban on the export of a specific class of data. While at the moment it is quite limited, it would not be inconsistent with the purposes of this Act to prohibit business TDF if the U.S. insists on having access to all data stored in U.S. data banks.

Domestic legislation and regulation that impacts on TDF is, currently limited in Canada. That which does exist affects only a small part of current or potential TDF; because of the indicated concerns in the areas of economic and cultural sovereignty as well as individual privacy, legislation in this area is most likely to be enlarged, creating a more regulated TDF environment.

D. *International Legal Influence on Domestic Regulation of TDF*

The paucity of domestic regulation concerning TDF, in turn, indicates that there is not a great influence from international sources. The impact of international legal sources is, however, felt to some extent in the domestic realm, especially where it concerns TDF in relation to individual privacy rights in data.

109 1980–1983 Can. Stat. ch. 111, § 60(1) (schedule I).
110 ONT. REV. STAT. ch. 56 (1980).
111 *Id.* at § 1.

Canada is a signatory of the (OECD) Guidelines Governing the Protection of Privacy and Transborder Flows of Personal Data.[112] These Guidelines set out the principles of national application as a guide for nations in protecting individual rights with respect to personal data gathering. Of more particular concern for TDF are the »Basic Principles of International Application: Free Flow and Legitimate Restrictions.«[113] These state:

> Member countries should take into consideration the implications for other Member countries of domestic processing and re-export of personal data, particularly where processing in one Member country would result in a circumvention or violation of the domestic legislation of other Member countries.
> Member countries should take all reasonable and appropriate steps to ensure that transborder flows of personal data, including transit through a Member country, are uninterrupted and secure.
> A Member country should refrain from restricting transborder flows of personal data between itself and another Member country except where the latter does not yet substantially observe these Guidelines.
> Member countries should refrain from developing laws, policies and practices in the name of the protection of privacy and individual liberties which, by exceeding requirements for the protection of privacy and individual liberties, are inconsistent with the free transborder flow of personal data.[114]

Prior to signing the Guidelines, Canada had been complying with them under the Access to Information and Privacy Act,[115] which followed the »Basic Principles of National Application« [116] in the implementation of personal data access and privacy, although only for public-sector data banks. Legislative regulation of the private sector has not been forthcoming, as the government, upon signing, has instead chosen to call for voluntary compliance by the private sector with the Guidelines.[117] The Act does not, however, specifically address the TDF issue. Instead it addresses rights of access by individuals to personal information that has come into the country from a foreign governmental source or is exported to a foreign government. Government-controlled personal information may be disclosed:

> (f) under an agreement or arrangement between the Government of Canada or an institution thereof and the government of a province, the government of a

112 OECD, Doc. C(80) 58 (final) (1980), *reprinted in* 20 I.L.M. 422 (1981).
113 *Id.* at part Three.
114 *Id.* at paras. 15–18.
115 1980–1983 Can.Stat. ch. 111.
116 OECD, *supra* note 112, at part Two.
117 There has already been favourable response to this. The Royal Bank of Canada declared that they would adopt the Guidelines in May 1984, just a week after Canada signed them. 7 TRANSNATIONAL DATA REPORT 297 (1984).

> foreign state, an international organization of states or an international organization established by the governments of states, or any institution of any such government, for the purpose of administering or enforcing any law or on carrying out a lawful investigation.[118]

On the other hand, according to section 19(1), any personal data given by, inter alia, a foreign government to a Canadian public-sector data bank may not be disclosed to the individual unless there is consent from the foreign government or that government has already made the information public.[119] With respect to public-sector holdings of personal data, the Guidelines have been used in Canada to establish certain legal restrictions both on outside access to that data and on personal access to it if the data has come from an outside governmental source. Again, this is applicable only to the public sector – the private sector has been left to self-regulation.

118 1980–1983 Can. Stat. ch. 111, § 8(2) (schedule II).
119 *Id.* at § 19(2).

Chapter IV: Regulation of the Markets for Network and Terminal Equipment

The regulation of the equipment market for remote data processing is the same as that for telephone services. Telecommunications in Canada is, as much as possible, regulated as a single entity (albeit by several legislatures), and the equipment market is one example of this regulatory policy. Reference should therefore be made to chapter II for an outline of the regulation of the equipment markets.

PART III: AUDIOVISUAL MEDIA PROGRAMS

The fear of »Americanization« is perhaps only one manifestation of the dilemma that exists in Canada as in many liberal democracies. In the name of freedom, are the means of communication to be operated by private owners with minimal intervention from public authorities? Or in the name of social responsibility, are controls to be placed on these keepers of the gates to promote or preserve some individual or collective good? Or should the state, as a legitimate representative of the public interest, assume through its agencies a positive communications role? In turn, Canada has answered yes to all of these questions, and no one would pretend that satisfactory answers to Canadian needs have been found. The search for a balance between national interests and broad cultural needs goes on.[120]

Chapter V: Introduction: Framework of National Law

The Canadian audiovisual media – for purposes of this study confined to television (TV), cable television (CATV) and direct-broadcast satellites (DBS) – is considered a single broadcasting system and, hence, regulated uniformly under federal laws, i.e., the Radio Act[121] and the Broadcasting Act.[122] The General Radio Regulations[123] adopted under the Radio Act[124] supplement the latters's provisions and provide detailed regulations governing the use of radio frequencies. The development of TV and CATV has resulted in the adoption under the Broadcasting Act[125] of specific detailed regulations to govern them – the Television Broadcasting Regulations[126] and the Cable Television Regulations.[127] On the other hand, direct broadcasting via satellites has not yet become operational, and no detailed regulations have been promulgated specifically to regulate this service. Some minor necessary changes have instead been made in the existing laws and regulations to extend their application to DBS. However, pressure is building in Canada to control this new technology, especially because of the rapid increase in »spill-over« of

120 Peers, *Canadian Media Regulation*, in STUDIES IN CANADIAN COMMUNICATIONS 73, 85 (1975).
121 CAN. REV. STAT. ch. R–1 (1970).
122 CAN. REV. STAT. ch. B–11 (1970).
123 CAN. CONSOL. REG. chs. 1371–72 (1978).
124 CAN. REV. STAT. ch. R–1, §§ 7–8 (1970).
125 CAN. REV. STAT. ch. B–11, § 16 (1970).
126 1964 CAN. STAT. O. & REGS. 50, *as amended*.
127 1975 CAN. STAT. O. & REGS. 665, *as amended by* CRTC Public Notice 1981–97 (Nov. 30, 1981).

transmissions of programs by U.S. satellites, both in the Fixed-Satellite Service (FSS) and the Broadcasting-Satellite Service (BSS).

The Canadian Constitution,[128] which established a federal form of government in Canada, is silent on the question of jurisdiction over broadcasting. However, through judicial interpretation of the Constitution, it is settled that jurisdiction lies with the federal government.[129]

The development of audiovisual media in Canada shows the influence both of Europe – because of the European heritage of a vast majority of Canadian people – and the U.S. – because of Canada's geographical proximity to this powerful country. In other words, Canadian audiovisual media is operated both as a public service to protect and enhance Canadian identity and as a private commercial enterprise to implement the capitalist democratic philosophy of Canada. The history of regulation of audiovisual media in Canada shows an effort to (a) control foreign programs, encourage Canadian content, and Canadianize this media, and (b) gradually privatize all forms of broadcasting.[130]

The presently applicable Broadcasting Act – a part of this effort – in section 3 sets forth the broadcasting policy for Canada. This policy establishes the essentials of Canadian audiovisual media regulation and, inter alia, provides that:

> (I) broadcasting undertakings in Canada constitute a single system comprising public and private elements;
>
> (II) the Canadian broadcasting system should be effectively owned and controlled by Canadians so as to safeguard, enrich and strengthen the cultural, political, social and economic fabric of Canada;
>
> (III) the right to freedom of expression and the right of persons to receive programs, subject only to generally applicable statutes and regulations, is unquestioned;
>
> (IV) the programming provided by each broadcaster should be of high standard, using predominantly Canadian creative and other resources;
>
> (V) there should be provided, through a corporation established by Parliament for the purpose, a national broadcasting service that is predominantly Canadian in content and character; and

128 British North America Act of 1967, 30 & 31 Vict., ch. 3, *as amended* (currently Constitution Act, 1867).

129 *See infra* pp. 62–65, 69–72.

130 For details, see generally R. BABE, CANADIAN TELEVISION BROADCASTING STRUCTURE, PERFORMANCE AND REGULATION (1979); D. ELLIS, EVOLUTION OF THE CANADIAN BROADCASTING SYSTEM: OBJECTIVES AND REALITIES – 1928–1968 (1979); F. PEERS, THE PUBLIC EYE: TELEVISION AND THE POLITICS OF CANADIAN BROADCASTING 1952–1968 (1979).

(VI) these objectives can best be achieved by providing for the regulation and supervision of the Canadian broadcasting system by a single independent public authority.

The Canadian Broadcasting Corporation (CBC) is the »corporation« referred to in (V) above and is governed by the provisions of Part III of the Broadcasting Act. The CRTC is the »single independent public authority« referred to in (VI) above. It operates under the provisions of Part II of the Broadcasting Act and under those of the Canadian Radio-television and Telecommunications Commission Act[131] and regulates broadcasting in Canada.

131 1974–1976 Can. Stat. ch. 49.

Chapter VI: Regulation of the Flow of Media Programs from Abroad

A. *International Law*

1. *International Telecommunications Law*

As stated in Part I, chapter I(A)(c) above, the rules of international law, which give rise to obligations between states, are transformed into Canadian national law according to the source of those rules. Customary rules of international law are considered to be a part of Canadian domestic law unless they conflict with Canadian statutory law. According to Macdonald, »customary rules of international law are adopted automatically into our law, amid a few caveats about sovereignty, and then directly applied unless they conflict with statute or some fundamental constitutional principle in which case legislation is required to enforce them.«[132] However, if the source of rules of international law is conventional, national legislative action – the ratification of a particular international treaty – is necessary to implement domestically the obligations undertaken by Canada. The Supreme Court in the *Capital Cities* case held that »[t]here would be no domestic internal consequences unless they arose from implementing legislation giving the Convention a legal effect within Canada.«[133]

The legislative jurisdiction to enact laws implementing an international broadcasting treaty lies with the federal legislature. In the *Radio Reference* case, the Privy Council held that in order for Canada to fulfill her treaty obligations, »it is necessary that the Dominion should pass legislation which would apply to all the dwellers in Canada.«[134] The authority to do so, according to the Privy Council, lies in section 91 of the Constitution Act,

132 Macdonald, *The Relationship Between International Law and Domestic Law in Canada*, in CANADIAN PERSPECTIVES ON INTERNATIONAL LAW AND ORGANISATION 111 (1974). This principle was first elucidated in Re Arrow River and Tributaries Slide & Boom Co., [1932] 2 D.L.R. 250, 260–61 (Can.).

133 *Capital Cities*, [1978] 2 S.C.R. 141, 173.

134 Re Regulation and Control of Radio Communication, 1932 A.C. 304, 313 (P.C.).

1867, which renders the powers of peace, order and good government to the federal government as opposed to the provincial governments. The *Radio Reference* case thus provided legal authority for federal jurisdiction over not only radio broadcasting but also TV and DBS. Because of the imperative use of radio waves for both TV and DBS, the jurisdiction of the federal government over them is clearly established.[135] However, the reasoning of the Supreme Court in *Capital Cities* is interesting as far as federal jurisdiction over CATV is concerned:

> The common sense of which the Privy Council spoke in the Radio case seems to me even more applicable here to prevent a situation of a divided jurisdiction in respect of the same signals or programmes according to whether they reach home television sets and the ultimate viewers through Hertzian waves or through coaxial cable.[136]

The federal jurisdiction over CATV was reaffirmed in the *Dionne v. Public Service Board (Quebec),*[137] in which the Supreme Court heavily relied upon *Capital Cities*.

The rules of international telecommunications law embodied in the International Telecommunication Convention (ITU Convention),[138] in the Radio Regulations appended to it[139] and in other treaties – like the 1937 Inter-American Radiocommunications Convention,[140] the 1983 Region 2 Plan regarding DBS,[141] and the 1952 Canadian-U.S.A. Television Agreement[142] – are implemented domestically by the federal government. The Federal Minister of Communications is required to secure the rights of Canada in telecommunications matters. According to section 8(1) of the Radio Act:[143]

> The Minister shall take such action as may be necessary to secure, by international regulation or otherwise, the rights of Her Majesty in right of Canada in telecommunications matters and shall consult the Canadian Radio-Television

135 For details, see Cooper, Satellite Telecommunication Law: The Canadian Perspective (unpublished LL.M. thesis submitted to the Faculty of Graduate Studies and Research, McGill University, in Montreal, 1984).

136 *Capital Cities*, [1978] 2 S.C.R. at 159.

137 [1978] 2 S.C.R. 191.

138 ITU Convention, *supra* note 1.

139 Radio Regulations, *supra* note 3.

140 Inter-American Radiocommunications Convention, Dec. 13, 1937, T.I.A.S. No. 4079.

141 *See* ITU, Final Acts of the Regional Administrative Conference for the Planning of the Broadcasting-Satellite Service in Region 2 (1983).

142 Agreement Concerning the Allocation of Television Channels, Apr. 23, 1952, Canada-United States, 1952 Can. T.S. No. 13 (*entered into force* June 23, 1952), *as amended by* Exchange of Notes, Feb. 26–Apr. 7, 1982, Canada-United States, T.I.A.S. No. 10645 (*entered into force* Apr. 7, 1982).

143 CAN. REV. STAT. ch. R–1 (1970).

Commission with respect to all such matters that, in his opinion, affect or concern broadcasting.

Pursuant to this duty, the Minister is entitled, under section 7(1) of the Radio Act, to make regulations »to carry out and make effective the terms of any international agreement, convention or treaty respecting telecommunications to which Canada is a party.« Pursuant to this authority, the Minister has issued the General Radio Regulations, Part II,[144] which contain detailed provisions with respect to the operation of radiocommunications. The operators of audiovisual media are obliged to observe the rules of international telecommunications law under section 10 of these Regulations. This section specifies that:

> The licensee shall observe the provisions of the International Telecommunication Convention and any bilateral or multilateral telecommunication agreements for the time-being in force and those regulations pertaining to the operation of radio that are made under the said Convention and agreements.[145]

The Minister is entitled to enforce the observance of rules of international telecommunications law on all broadcasting undertakings, including CATV and DBS; this is accomplished through the requirement that they obtain a technical construction and operating certificate from the Minister before starting their operations.[146]
Through this process, which will be discussed in detail below, international telecommunications law becomes the domestic law of Canada. However, where an international treaty has not been domestically implemented, it cannot have legal effect in Canada. In other words, the extent of Canada's international obligation to allow access to its territory for foreign programs depends on the domestic implementation of the treaties or agreements that created those international obligations. Since all licensees are required to observe the provisions of the ITU Convention, they are, therefore, prohibited from causing intentionally harmful interference with (i.e., jamming) the broadcasting stations that operate in accordance with the provisions of the ITU Convention and the Radio Regulations.[147] There is nothing in the Radio

144 CAN. CONSOL. REG. ch. 1372 (1978).
145 *Id.* at § 10.
146 Radio Act. CAN. REV. STAT. ch. R–1, §§ 4(b)(ii), 5 (1970). For details, *see infra* pp. 98–103.
147 Article 35 of the ITU Convention, *supra* note 1, obliges all member-states to operate all of their radio stations in such a manner as not to cause harmful interference to the radio services or communications of other members.

Act or the Broadcasting Act that authorises the Canadian government to jam television or DBS signals of foreign origin.

Television broadcasting stations within 250 miles of the Canada-U.S. border, where the majority of the Canadian population lives, are operated in accordance with a U.S.-Canada bilateral television agreement. The agreement contains no provisions restricting the reception of U.S. television signals in Canada. In the case of DBS, while unintentional »spill-over« is accepted, Canada subscribes to the view that international direct-broadcasting service should be operated in accordance with paragraph No. 2674 of the ITU Radio Regulations,[148] i.e., on the basis of a prior agreement/agreements between the transmitting and receiving countries.[149] Also, as discussed below, CATV companies in Canada are not allowed to receive more than four foreign television channels.

Technical standards, internationally adopted through the ITU, are implemented in Canada through the above-mentioned section 10 of the General Radio Regulations. The import and sale of radio apparatus capable of receiving television broadcasting for use in Canada after May 31, 1969 comes under the 1952 U.S.-Canada TV agreement by way of section 130 of the General Radio Regulations, Part II.

2. *International Human Rights Conventions*

Canada has ratified a considerable number of international conventions on human rights.[150] However for our present discussion, the International Covenant on Civil and Political Rights (hereinafter, the Covenant) is the

148 Article 30(3) (No. 2674) of the ITU Radio Regulations, *supra* note 3, specifies: »In devising the characteristics of a space station in the broadcasting-satellite service, all technical means available shall be used to reduce, to the maximum extent practicable, the radiation over the territory of other countries unless an agreement has been previously reached with such countries.«

149 For details, see Chapman & Warren, *Direct Broadcast Satellites: the ITU, the U.N. and the Real World*, 4 ANNALS OF AIR & SPACE L. 413 (1979).

150 These include: International Convenant on Economic, Social and Cultural Rights, *in force for Canada* Aug. 19, 1976, 1976 Can. T.S. No. 46; International Convenant on Civil and Political Rights (and Optional Protocol), *in force for Canada* Aug. 19, 1976, 1976 Can. T.S. No. 47; International Convention on the Elimination of All Forms of Racial Discrimination, *in force for Canada* Nov. 13, 1970, 1970 Can. T.S. No. 28; and Convention on the Elimination of All Forms of Discrimination Against Women, *in force for Canada* Jan. 10, 1982, U.N. Doc. A/RES/34/180.

relevant and most important convention. The Covenant has been in force for Canada since August 19, 1976. Canada has also ratified the Optional Protocol to the Covenant, which in article 1 states that any individual subject to the jurisdiction of a state party to the Convenant who claims to be a victim of a violation by the government of that state of any of the rights guaranteed in the Covenant can complain to the Human Rights Committee established under article 28 of the Covenant.

As noted earlier, a treaty must be implemented domestically by specifically appropriate legislation in order for its provisions to be incorporated into Canadian law. The federal government has the power to implement an international treaty domestically if the subject matter of the treaty is within its jurisdictional powers. There is no specific Canadian legislation implementing the Convenant in Canada.

The Canadian Charter of Rights and Freedoms (hereinafter, the Charter)[151] and the Broadcasting Act, both of which contain some provisions similar to article 19 of the Covenant, include no specific reference to the Covenant and were never adopted because of Canada's ratification of the Covenant. In the Canadian legal system, therefore, the Covenant has the status of a ratified but unimplemented treaty.[152]

However,

> it must be emphasised that in order to fulfill obligations under the Covenant, it is not necessary to incorporate the Covenant directly into the constitution or laws of the ratifying state. ... Therefore, it is not necessary that every single right and freedom set out in articles 1 to 27 of the Covenant is specified in the laws or the constitution of a State Party, because a violation occurs only when a standard of the Covenant is contravened, not when a State Party fails to incorporate the provisions of the Covenant.[153]

Specific provisions of the Covenant can be seen as having been indirectly implemented. For example, section 2(b) of the Charter, as well as section 3(c) of the Broadcasting Act, contain provisions similar to those in article 19 of the Covenant. Section 2 of the Charter states that »[e]veryone has the following fundamental freedoms ... (b) freedom of thought, belief, opinion and expression, including freedom of the press and other media of communi-

151 For the text of the Charter, see Constitution Act, 1982, part I, ch. 11

152 For details, see Cohen & Bayefsky, *The Canadian Charter of Rights and Freedoms and Public International Law*, 61 CAN. BAR REV. 264, 302 (1983); Tarnopolsky, *A Comparison Between the Canadian Charter of Rights and Freedoms and the International Convenant on Civil and Political Rights*, 8 QUEEN'S L.J. 211, 213 (1982–83).

153 Tarnopolsky, *supra* note 152, at 212.

cation.«[154] Similary, section 3(c) of the Broadcasting Act specifies that »the right to freedom of expression and the right of persons to receive programs, subject only to generally applicable statutes and regulations, is unquestioned.« Article 19 of the Covenant, on the other hand, provides that:

1. Everyone shall have the right to hold opinions without interference.
2. Everyone shall have the right to freedom of expression; this right shall include freedom to seek, receive and impart information and ideas of all kinds, regardless of frontiers, either orally, in writing or in print, in the form of art, or through any other media of this choice.
3. The exercise of the rights provided for in paragraph 2 of this article carries with it special duties and responsibilities. It may therefore be subject to certain restrictions, but these shall only be such as are provided by law and are necessary:
   (a) For respect of the rights or reputations of others;
   (b) For the protection of national security or of public order (*ordre public*), or of public health or morals.

The extent of transformation of the provisions of article 19 of the Covenant depends upon its impact in the interpretation of the above-mentioned provisions of the Charter and the Broadcasting Act. Being a part of an unimplemented treaty, article 19 has no legal force in Canada.[155] However, in the application of relevant provisions of the Charter and the Broadcasting Act, article 19 can be used by Canadian courts as an interpretative aid because there is presumption that Parliament and the legislatures, unless doing so by express word, do not intend to legislate in violation of Canada's treaty obligations.[156] According to Claydon, »unimplemented treaties, and norms emanating from international intergovernmental agencies can play a potentially significant role in supplementing ambiguous domestic law or in justifying interpretations derived from domestic sources.«[157] Because of this, article 19 of the Covenant may play an interpretive role in the judicial development of section 2(6) of the Charter.

However, in the Canadian legal system, even a ratified and implemented treaty has no legal effect if it contradicts an unambiguous Canadian statute.

154 This freedom should be read in light of section 1 of the Charter, which provides that »[t]he Canadian Charter of Rights and Freedoms guarantees the rights and freedoms set out in it subject only to such reasonable limits prescribed by law as can be demonstrably justified in a free and democratic society.«

155 Claydon, *International Human Rights Law and the Interpretation of the Canadian Charter of Rights and Freedoms*, 4 SUP. CT. L. REV. 287, 294 (1982).

156 *Id.* at 295. *See also* articles cited *supra* note 152.

157 Claydon, *The Application of International Human Rights Law by Canadian Courts*, 30 BUFFALO L. REV. 727, 737 (1981).

»There is no doubt in Canada that where the domestic legislation cannot be given a possible meaning in conformity with the treaty it is the domestic legislation which will take effect.«[158] The use of unimplemented treaties in interpreting domestic legislation is limited by the fact that an ambiguity in that legislation must first be established. In the *Capital Cities* case, the late Chief Justice Bora Laskin, speaking for the majority, stated that he would not consider the Inter-American Radiocommunications Convention of 1937 in interpreting the Broadcasting Act because he did »not find any ambiguity that would require resort to the Convention.«[159]

In addition to article 19, article 20 of the Covenant contains important provisions that have some relevance to audiovisual media in Canada. Article 20 provides that: »(1) Any propaganda for war shall be prohibited by law. (2) Any advocacy of national, racial or religious hatred that constitutes incitement to discrimination, hostility or violence shall be prohibited by law.« While sections 281.1, 281.2 and 281.3 of the Criminal Code[160] contain provisions sufficient to meet the requirements of article 20(2), there is no law in Canada that specifically prohibits propaganda for war. According to a Canadian governmental report, »an individual or organisation may, therefore, legally disseminate such propaganda. The Government of Canada cannot do so, however, without breaking the commitments it made by signing the Covenant.«[161]

Jurisdiction for the application of the rules of relevant human rights conventions to audiovisual media lies with the federal government because of its legislative jurisdiction over all kinds of broadcasting in Canada. Because of the rather limited scope of international human rights law, its application in Canada has been negligible. However, the right to receive foreign programs, as specified in the Broadcasting Act, has been given effect in some cases, not as part of international law but of domestic law; hence, it will be discussed

158 Cohen & Bayefsky, *supra* note 152, at 295. This rule, however, is at odds with a rule of international law that holds that a state cannot rely upon its domestic law to avoid its international legal obligations. *But see infra* n. 159.

159 [1978] 2 S.C.R. at 173. The late Chief Justice Laskin further stated that »certainly the Convention per se cannot prevail against the express stipulations of the Act.« *Id.* Similarly, the Federal Court of Appeal in A.G. Canada v. Stuart, 137 D.L.R.3d 740, 748–49 (Fed. C.A. 1982), stated that the Convention on the Elimination of Discrimination Against Women »cannot be used by this Court in construing and interpreting sections of the Unemployment Insurance Act particularly in cases where a definitive interpretation has been made by the Supreme Court of Canada.«

160 CAN. REV. STAT. ch. C-34, *as amended* (1970).

161 DEPARTMENT OF SECRETARY OF STATE, INTERNATIONAL COVENANT ON CIVIL AND POLITICAL RIGHTS: REPORT OF CANADA ON IMPLEMENTATION OF THE PROVISIONS OF THE COVENANT 86–87 (1979).

below. That too evidences judicial recourse against regulatory decisions that deny the application of human rights in Canada.

3. *Summary*

International telecommunications and human rights laws in fact have little impact on Canada's sovereign right to regulate the access of audiovisual programs broadcast into its territory, because international treaties, ratified by Canada, have no legal effect unless implemented by specific legislation. Furthermore, a ratified and implemented treaty cannot prevail against the express and unambiguous stipulation of a statute. Ratified treaties (implemented or unimplemented) can be used only as an aid in the interpretation and application of domestic legislation and only when an ambiguity has first been established.

B. *National Law*

1. *Domestic Media and its Regulation*

The constitutional basis regarding powers to regulate and the essentials of the Canadian audiovisual media has already been mentioned above.[162] It may, however, be added that – since it is difficult to make a distinction between the media and the contents of a program – courts in Canada have settled almost exclusive jurisdiction over the contents of all forms of broadcasting with the federal government.

For example, in *Re C.F.R.B. and A.G. of Canada,*[163] the Ontario Court of Appeal extended the reasoning of the Privy Council in the *Radio Reference* case to allow federal jurisdiction over not only the physical means of communication (carrier) but also the program content. The issue was settled

162 *See supra* pp. 59–65.
163 [1973] 3 Ont. 819.

in the *Capital Cities*[164] case, where the Supreme Court decided that the CRTC – a federal agency – was entitled to regulate the content of broadcasting in order to prevent a situation of divided jurisdiction. However, exclusive federal jurisdiction over broadcasting content was somewhat tempered by the Supreme Court in the later case of *A.G.of Quebec v. Kellogg's Co. of Canada.*[165] It declared the Quebec Consumer Protection Act[166] – a provincial law – *intra vires*. The Court stated that the Quebec law, which restricted the use by advertisers of cartoons in broadcasting advertising targeted at children, was in fact directed at the advertiser and not the broadcaster, thus giving the province indirect control over some broadcast content.

In contrast to audiovisual media, the regulation of newspapers, magazines and other print media has been limited. This is so because of Canada's democratic tradition and consequent avoidance of governmental interference with freedom of speech and expression and freedom of the press.[167] The Canadian Bill of Rights[168] in section 1 »recognised and declared that in Canada there have existed and shall continue to exist ... human rights and fundamental freedoms, namely, ... freedom of speech, ... and freedom of the press.« These freedoms have been reiterated in section 2 of the Canadian Charter of Rights and Freedoms.

Though neither the federal nor the provincial governments have primary jurisdiction over the print media, both levels of government have passed laws that apply to this form of media. Under the Constitution, Parliament may make laws with respect to criminal activities, certain commercial activities, such as foreign investment, and national security. On the other hand, provincial jurisdiction over the regulation of trade and commerce within a province is predominant, extending also to commercial transaction and marketing activities and civil rights within a province.[169]

The essential feature of print-media regulation is that it has been the least regulated communications industry in Canada. The only example of press censorship in recent Canadian history occurred during the October Crisis in

164 [1978] 2 S.C.R. 141.
165 [1978] 2 S.C.R. 211.
166 QUE. REV. STAT. ch. P–40 (1977).
167 For details, see Tarnopolsky, *Freedom of the Press*, in 3 NEWSPAPERS AND THE LAW 1 (1980).
168 An Act for the Recognition and Protection of Human Rights and Fundamental Freedoms, 8 & 9 Eliz. 2, ch. 44 (assented to Aug. 10, 1960).
169 For details, see Beaudoin, *Newspapers and Constitutional Competence*, in 3 NEWSPAPERS AND THE LAW 75 (1980).

1970, when the federal government, under the War Measures Act,[170] prohibited the publication of anything that threatened national security.[171] Sections 260 to 280 and 159 of the Criminal Code make it an indictable offence to publish anything defamatory or obscene. These provisions, which have been extensively applied by the courts, are considered legitimate restrictions on the freedom of the press.[172]

Perhaps the most important governmental involvement in the print media has been the 1965 amendment to the Income Tax Act, protecting Canadian magazines against foreign competition and preventing foreign ownership of Canadian newspapers. During the early 1960s, American magazines, especially *Time* and *Reader's Digest*, were flooding the Canadian market, and Canadian magazines were being squeezed under the resulting heavy competition. According to the Royal Commission on Publications, which was appointed to investigate the situation, Canadians were »exposed increasingly to a vast network of communications which reaches to every corner of our land; American words, images and print – the good, the bad and the indifferent – batter unrelentingly ... at our eyes and ears.«[173] The Commission reported that *Time* and *Reader's Digest* were receiving over 40 percent of the total magazine advertising revenue in Canada and recommended the disallowance of deductions from income tax by a taxpayer for expenditures incurred for advertising directed at the Canadian market in a foreign periodical.[174]

To protect the Canadian magazine industry, the federal government amended the Income Tax Act and thereby prohibited business-expense deductions for income-tax purposes of the cost of advertisements, if these advertisements were published in non-Canadian newspapers and magazines that were primarily aimed at Canadian readers.[175] It defined a Canadian publication as one that was printed, edited, typeset and published in Canada. Moreover, in order for a corporation publishing in Canada to be considered Canadian under the law, its ownership and direction must be 75 percent Canadian and incorporated in Canada. This provision proved an effective block to foreign ownership of Canadian print media. However, since *Time* and *Reader's Digest* had

170 CAN. REV. STAT. ch. W–2 (1970).

171 1970 CAN. STAT. O. & REGS. 444, § 4.

172 *See* Tarnopolsky, *supra* note 167, at 16–35. *See also* C. BECKTON, THE LAW AND THE MEDIA IN CANADA 23–58, 141–58 (1982).

173 REPORT OF THE ROYAL COMMISSION ON PUBLICATIONS 5–6 (1961). The Commission further observed that the »per annum circulation of United States business papers in Canada rose 309 per cent between 1950 and 1959, while Canadian business papers rose only 88 per cent.« *Id.* at 26.

174 *Id.* at 88.

175 1965 Can. Stat. ch. 18, § 4.

established branch operations in Canada to distribute their Canadian editions, they were exempted from the application of the new section 12A of the Income Tax Act. They achieved this exemption because of their effective lobbying and with the support of the U.S. State Department.[176] Thus, they continued their hegemony in Canadian magazine market to the extent that, by 1969, they had gained the largest circulation in Canada.

In 1969 the Special Senate Committee on Mass Media proposed the removal of the income tax exemption for these magazines[177] and stated:

> Somehow or other, we've arrived in the peculiarly Canadian position where our most successful magazines are American magazines, and we're moving inexorably toward the day when they'll be the *only* magazines we have. This may make sense in terms of economics; on every other basis it's intolerable.[178]

No step, however, was taken to implement the Committee's proposal.

Frank W. Peers seems to have rightly summed up our discussion on print media with his remark that »[e]xcept in the field of broadcasting, regulation of Canadian media of communications has been limited to a general proscription in the criminal code against libel and obscenity, and a few belated attempts to protect Canadian publications against the diversion of advertising revenue to foreign periodicals.«[179]

2. *General Laws Applicable to Audiovisual Media*

Audiovisual media as an enterprise is subject to national (federal, provincial and municipal) laws regulating business activities in general, e.g., business licenses, taxes, labour relations, etc. Since they are relatively less important in the context of the present study, they are not analysed here. However, some national laws are of direct relevance to audiovisual media, and they deserve some discussion. These relate particularly to defamation, libel, hate propaganda, obscenity, advertising and antitrust activities.

176 Peers, *supra* note 120, at 84.
177 SPECIAL SENATE COMMITTEE ON MASS MEDIA, I REPORT ON MASS MEDIA 256 (1970).
178 *Id.*
179 Peers, *supra* note 120, at 73.

a) *Defamation*

Defamation is an attack upon the moral character or personality of a person, attributing to him or her any form of disgrace. In Canada, each province has jurisdiction over defamation actions, and most provinces have passed defamation or libel and slander acts.[180] Defamation actions are also governed by common law. The term »defamation« includes the concepts of both slander and libel. »Slander« is the spoken word or words in a nonpermanent form, while »libel« is the written word or words in a permanent form. However, with the advent of TV, it has become difficult to distinguish between the two concepts, because a speech on TV may be of a transient nature but has a great potential to damage reputation. Slander at common law requires proof of special damages, whereas libel is actionable without such proof. Libel implies both civil and criminal liability. The criminal-law aspect of libel will be discussed in section (b) below.

To be successful in a defamation suit, the plaintiff must prove that the alleged words were defamatory in their ordinary and natural meaning, that they referred to him and that they were published. Publication includes broadcast on radio and TV. Defences against the charges of defamation, the burden of proof of which lies with the defendant, include absolute privilege, qualified privilege, fair comment, justification and consent. A plaintiff who alleges that his reputation has been damaged by the defamatory words of the defendant may claim pecuniary damages. Apology on the part of the defendant may mitigate the damages but is not accepted as a defence at common law.[181]

In the case where the defamatory words are broadcast in Canada and the person whose reputation they damage also lives in Canada, no problem arises with respect to the jurisdiction of a Canadian court to hear that case. However, if the broadcast containing defamatory words originates in a foreign country, e.g., the U.S., and is watched via TV, CATV or DBS by a person in Canada whose reputation is damaged by that broadcast, a question arises as to whether that person has a cause of action against the U.S. broadcaster and whether a Canadian court will hear that case. The answer to this question lies in the determination of whether the publication occurred in Canada. In the case of *Jenner v. Sun Oil Co.*,[182] the Ontario Court held that since the broadcast had been heard in Ontario (Canada), it could be concluded that publication had taken place in Ontario. Thus, in reverse, a statement

180 *See, e.g.*, the Ontario Libel and Slander Act, ONT. REV. STAT. ch. 237 (1980).
181 For a detailed discussion, see C. BECKTON, *supra* note 172, at 26–48.
182 1952 Ont. 240 (H.C.)

broadcast in Ontario could be the subject of a libel action in Michigan (U.S.) if heard there.

b) *Libel*

A defamatory statement may endanger public peace and welfare and thus is considered a criminal offence under the Criminal Code. The Code contains provisions regarding seditious and blasphemous or defamatory libel.
Under section 62 of the Code, anyone who speaks seditious words or publishes a seditious libel is guilty of an indictable offence. Seditious libel is a libel that expresses a seditious intention, and everyone is presumed to have a seditious intention who teaches, advocates or publishes the use, without the authority of law, of force as a means of accomplishing a governmental change in Canada.[183] However, a person cannot be presumed to have a seditious intention under certain circumstances enumerated in section 61 of the Code.
Similarly, anyone who publishes a blasphemous libel is guilty of an indictable offence under section 260 of the Code. Without specifically defining the term »blasphemous libel,« the section states that it is a question of fact whether particular published matter is a blasphemous libel. However, a person cannot be convicted of an offence under this section for expressing, in good faith and in decent language, an opinion upon a religious subject.
A defamatory libel is matter published without lawful justification or excuse that is likely to injure the reputation of any person.[184] Such a libel may be expressed either directly or by insinuation or irony. A person publishes a libel when he exhibits it in public, causes it to be read or seen, or shows or causes it to be shown, with the intent that it should be seen by the person whom it defames or by any other person.[185] Defamatory libel is an indictable offence. Intentional defamatory libel is punishable by imprisonment for five years; unintentional defamatory libel, for two years.[186] Publication includes broadcasting via any audiovisual media, and, in light of *Jenner v. Sun Oil Co.*, a foreign broadcaster should be indicted in Canada if his libelous broadcast were seen in Canada.

183 CAN. REV. STAT. ch. C–34, § 60 *as amended* (1970).
184 *Id.* at § 262.
185 *Id.* at § 263.
186 *Id.* at §§ 264–65.

c) *Hate Propaganda*

The Criminal Code prohibits hate propaganda against any group that can be distinguished by colour, race, religion or ethnic origin. Sections 281.1 and 281.2 of the Code prohibit incitement to genocide or hatred. Hate propaganda means communicating statements, in any public place, that incite hatred against any identifiable group, where such incitement is likely to lead to a breach of peace. »Communicating« includes communicating by broadcasting or other audible or visible means. »Public place« includes any place to which the public has access as of right or by invitation, either express or implied. »Statements« include words spoken or recorded electronically or electromagnetically or otherwise, and gestures, signs and other visible representations.[187] Therefore, it is clear that hate propaganda by all audiovisual media (TV, CATV, DBS) is prohibited under the Criminal Code. This prohibition applies to Canadian audiovisual media as well as to foreign media, where it can be established that it has the effect of »communicating« in Canada.
As noted earlier, sections 281.1 to 281.3 give effect to article 20(2) of the International Covenant on Civil and Political Rights, to which Canada is a party. However, since in Canada there is no specific law giving effect to article 20(1) of the Covenant, an individual or organization may therefore legally broadcast propaganda in favour of war.

(d) *Obscenity*

According to section 159(8) of the Criminal Code, »any publication a dominant characteristic of which is the undue exploitation of sex, or sex and any one or more of the following subjects, namely, crime, horror, cruelty and violence, shall be deemed to be obscene.«
A person is guilty of an offence if he publishes, or has in his possession for the purpose of publication, any obscene matter, picture, model or other thing whatsoever.[188] Similarly, an offence is committed when a person knowingly and without lawful justification or excuse (a) exposes to public view any obscene matter or other thing whatsoever, (b) publicly exhibits a disgusting object or an indecent show or (c) advertises or publishes an advertisement of any means, instructions, medicine, drug or article intended or represented as a

187 *Id.* at § 281.2(7).
188 *Id.* at § 159(1).

method of causing abortion or miscarriage, etc.[189] For the purposes of section 159, the motives of an accused are irrelevant, and the ignorance of the obscene nature of the material is no excuse. However, a person cannot be convicted of an offence if he establishes that the public good was served by the acts that are alleged to constitute the offence.[190]

In *R. v. Rioux*,[191] the Supreme Court held that if a person showed obscene movies to ten persons in the privacy of his home, he did not »circulate« or »distribute« obscene material within the meaning of section 159. According to the Court »›[c]irculation‹ must involve some public element by the fact that, in the same section, the term ›circulation‹ is juxtaposed with the word ›distribution‹.«[192] Therefore, TV, CATV and DBS, whose signals are directed at the public, may in fact »circulate« or »distribute« within the meaning of section 159.

The definition of obscenity was added to section 159(8) in 1959[193] to replace what was known as the subjective test established in *R. v. Hicklin* in England in 1868.[194] The present definition of obscenity establishes the objective test, and »undue exploitation of sex« must be determined in the context of community standards and with consideration of the seriousness of the purpose of the author or producer.[195] The degree of obscenity of a particular matter depends upon the media used for its exposure to the public; in other words, »what may be tolerated and so acceptable in a legitimate theatre may not be tolerated when another medium, for example, television, is utilized ... where there is mass and indiscriminate availability of a wide variety of viewers of all ages and interests who may unwittingly be exposed to such [obscene] material.«[196] Therefore, a standard to judge the obscenity of matter made public through TV, CATV and DBS will be more rigorous than one for matter that is shown in a theatre.

Under section 5(1) of its Television Broadcasting Regulations, the CRTC requires that every broadcasting station or network operator not broadcast »any obscene, indecent or profane language or pictorial presentation.«[197]

189 *Id.* at § 159(2).
190 *Id.* at § 159(3).
191 [1970] 3 Can. Crim. Cases 149.
192 *Id.* at 156.
193 An Act to Amend the Criminal Code, 1959 Can. Stat. ch. 41, § 11.
194 [1868] 3 Q.B. 360, 371. The *Hicklin* test determines »whether the tendency of the matter charged as obscene is to deprave and corrupt those minds that are open to such immoral influences, and into whose hands a publication of this sort might fall.«
195 *See* Brodie, Dansky & Rubin v. The Queen, 1962 S.C.R. 681.
196 R. v. O'Reilly, [1970] 3 Ont. 429, 442, 1 Can. Crim. Cases 2d 24, 38. *See also* R. v. Sudbury News Ltd., 18 Ont.2d, 428, 435 (1978).
197 1964 CAN. STAT. O. & REGS. 50, *as amended*.

While the CRTC is not a censorship body and leaves it to the courts to define obscenity,[198] it can revoke, suspend or refuse to renew the license of a broadcaster who has failed to comply with the conditions laid down in section 5(1).[199]

e) *Advertising*

Under section 16(1) of the Broadcasting Act, the CRTC may make regulations respecting the character of and the amount of time that may be devoted to advertising. Pursuant to this provision, the CRTC has issued regulations under the Television Broadcasting Regulations that restrict the amount of advertising time permitted but do not greatly restrict the character of advertising. No station or network operator is permitted during any clock hour to broadcast programming containing advertising material the aggregate duration of which exceeds 12 minutes.[200]

Television stations are not allowed to advertise any thing or matter for the purpose of promoting any act or thing prohibited by the law of Canada or of the province in which the station is located.[201] There are special provisions with respect to advertising of spirituous liquors, beer, wine, cider, food and drugs; advertisements for these products must be approved by the CRTC.[202] The Commission has also placed »conditions on the licenses of broadcasters requiring adherence to the Broadcast Code for Advertising to Children, which in turn requires preclearance by the Children's Section of the Advertising Standards Council and *le Conseil des normes de la publicité*, of all broadcast advertising directed to children.«[203]

In 1984 in Canada, $5.6 billion was spent on advertising all media, and television accounted for $1 billion.[204] To promote the Canadian production of television commercials, the CRTC has adopted regulations under which a registration number is assigned to a commercial message upon receiving

198 CRTC, STATEMENT CONCERNING FIRST CHOICE PAY TELEVISION PROGRAMMING (Public Notice 1983–16) (1983).

199 Broadcasting Act, CAN. REV. STAT. B–11, §§ 16(1)(c), 17(1)(d), 22, 24 (1970).

200 1964 CAN. STAT. O. & REGS. 50, § 8(1), *as amended*

201 *Id.* at § 9(1).

202 *Id.* at §§ 10–11.

203 CRTC, BROADCAST ADVERTISING HANDBOOK: ACTS, REGULATIONS AND GUIDELINES ON BROADCAST ADVERTISING 1 (1978).

204 *Where Advertising Dollars Go*, Montreal Gazette, Apr. 19, 1985, at B–1.

required information. This establishes a method by which the CRTC can assess the degree of Canadian content existing in commercials.[205]

To reduce the economic impact of the penetration of U.S. television stations in Canada and in order to enhance the capability of the Canadian broadcasting system to achieve national broadcasting objectives found in section 3 of the Broadcasting Act, the CRTC has the power to allow CATV operators to remove commercials from incoming U.S. TV signals and replace them with their own.[206] The CATV operators are not allowed to broadcast any advertising material on their channels reserved for community programming.[207]

f) *Antitrust Activities*

To assure the public the benefits of competition, Parliament passed the Combines Investigation Act,[208] which prohibits combines, mergers or the formation of monopolies that unduly restrain or injure competition. The Act covers both goods and services. However, according to Cody-Rice, the »Canadian courts have not taken a very aggressive attitude toward the prevention of monopoly control and sections 2 and 33 of the Act have been emasculated by judicial interpretation so that they are now essentially useless in dealing with any industry.«[209] The ideological role of the audiovisual media has been recognised in the Broadcasting Act. The federal government has formulated a policy that it applies to the communications industry to protect the interests of the general public: the industry should be »effectively owned and controlled by Canadians so as to safeguard, enrich and strengthen the cultural, political, social, and economic fabric of Canada.«[210]

The CRTC has extensive powers under the Broadcasting Act to investigate the operations of broadcast companies to ensure that the above-mentioned objective of the Act is being achieved. Under section 16(1)(b), of the Act, the CRTC is empowered to promulgate regulations »requiring licensees to submit to the Commission such information regarding their programs and financial affairs or otherwise relating to the conduct and management of their affairs ...

205 For details, see CRTC, *supra* note 203, at 12–14. In a public announcement on Jan. 12, 1976, the CTRC stated it hoped to achieve a Canadian content of nearly 80% in TV commercials.
206 CRTC Public Announcement, Jan. 21, 1977. *See also Capital Cities*, [1978] 2 S.C.R. 141.
207 Cable Television Regulations, 1975 CAN. STAT. O. & REGS. 665, § 11, *as amended.*
208 CAN. REV. STAT. ch. C–23, *as amended by* 1974–1976 Can. Stat. ch. 76.
209 Cody-Rice, *The Treatment of the Term »To the Detriment or Against the Interest of the Public«*, in 3 NEWSPAPERS AND THE LAW 103, 142 (1980).
210 Broadcasting Act, CAN. REV. STAT. B–11, § 3(b) (1970).

and respecting such other matters as it deems necessary for the furtherance of its objectives.« The CRTC requires that its approval be obtained prior to transferring ownership or effective control of licensed broadcasting undertakings. The means by which this general requirement of prior approval has been imposed is the stipulation in each case of a condition of license to that effect. Where a licensee is incorporated as a private company, a further condition requires that the prior approval of the CRTC be obtained for the transfer of that licensee's stock.[211]

With respect to the cross-ownership of media, CRTC's policy does not favour it: »[i]n numerous decisions dating back to 1969, the Commission has, directly and by implication, expressed its opinion that except in special circumstances television undertakings should be independent of cable television undertakings, both as regards ownership and control and as regards substantial shareholdings.«[212]

Similarly, the CRTC considers that ownership and control of broadcasting and newspapers should be separate except in special circumstances.[213] This policy has been supported by the federal government. For the general purpose of fostering independent, competitive and diverse sources of news and viewpoints within Canada, the federal government issued a directive to the CRTC under article 22(1) of the Broadcasting Act, whereby »with certain exceptions, enterprises engaged in the publication of daily newspapers shall be prohibited from owning or controlling broadcasting undertakings operating in the same market area.«[214]

Though this directive has only been in force for about two years and applied in just six cases, doubts have been expressed with respect to the viability of the directive in achieving the desired goal of diverse and competitive sources of news and views via the diversification of the ownership of broadcasting media in Canada.[215] On the other hand, the CRTC has expressed its willingness to relax cross-ownership restrictions, not only in the cases of cross-ownership of newspapers and broadcast stations but also for the cross-ownership of cable and TV stations, if that is what it takes to ensure the financial strength and survival of the Canadian broadcasting system.[216]

211 General Radio Regulations, Part II (Special Regulations Applicable to Private Commercial Broadcasting Stations), CAN. CONSOL. REG. chs. 1371–72, § 115(4); CRTC, Public Announcement, Jan. 7, 1980.

212 CRTC, CONCENTRATION OF OWNERSHIP IN PRIVATE BROADCASTING: THE QUESTION OF CROSS-OWNERSHIP (Notice of Public Hearing, Feb. 9, 1979).

213 *Id.*

214 1982 CAN. STAT. O. & REGS. 746.

215 For details, see Townsend, *Regulation of Newspaper/Broadcasting, Media Cross-Ownership in Canada*, 33 UNIV. N.B.L.J. 261 (1984).

216 *CRTC Says It's Willing to Ease Ownership Rules*, Montreal Gazette, Apr. 4, 1985, at D–1.

3. *Canadian Law and Incoming Foreign Programs*

Canadian regulations controlling incoming foreign programs are the result of Canada's serious concerns over the protection of its cultural and economic sovereignty. Before we discuss these regulations, it is necessary to look at the economic importance of broadcasting in Canada and the magnitude of the influence of foreign programs on the Canadian population.

According to a Canadian governmental publication,[217] the Canadian telecommunications industry generates operating revenues of $7.8 billion per year and employs more than 125,000 people. This represents about 3% of the gross domestic product (GDP) and makes it the largest high-technology employer. During the period between 1971 and 1981, the operating revenues of the cultural sector – comprising publishing firms, film and videotape production and broadcasting – grew significantly faster than the GDP. In 1981 the total contribution to the GDP of this sector exceeded $2.7 billion, almost 1% of the GDP. This means that the cultural sector contributed just a little less to the Canadian economy than did the textile, aircraft and chemical industries combined. During this ten-year period, the number of people working in cultural occupations doubled, as compared with a growth rate of 30% for all occupations. This shows the increasing importance of telecommunications and cultural industries to overall economic performance in Canada.

The Canadian broadcasting industry's 1984-85 revenues approached $3 billion, including $905 million for the Canadian Broadcasting Corporation (CBC), which employs about 75,000 people, directly and indirectly.[218]

Canadians spend nearly 500 million hours per week watching TV, i.e., about 23 hours per person per week. A child of 12 years of age is estimated to have spent nearly 12,000 hours watching TV – about twice as much time as he has spent in a class room.[219]

217 F. Fox, Culture and Communications: Key Elements of Canada's Economic Future (brief submitted by the former Minister of Communications to the Royal Commission on the Economic Union and Development Prospects for Canada, in Montreal, Nov. 3, 1983) at 6, 13.

218 M. Masse, The Canadian Broadcasting System: Into the Twenty-First Century (notes for an address by the Minister of Communications to the Canadian Cable Television Association and the Broadcast Executives Society, in Toronto, Apr. 9, 1984) at 7.

219 F. Fox, Radiotélédiffusion et souveraineté culturelle (notes pour une allocation du Ministre des Communications devant l'Association du Commonwealth pour la Radiodiffusion, in Toronto, June 13, 1982) at 6. *See also Technology Likely to Tighten Foreign Grip on CBC: Juneau*, Montreal Gazette, Nov. 1, 1982, at C–1; *CBC Chief Warns U.S. TV Could »Swamp« Canada*, Montreal Gazette, June 14, 1980, at 12.

The CRTC Policy Statement on Canadian Content in Television[220] states that:

> [F]oreign programs account for 77 per cent of the total viewing of English-language television programs over the entire day and 85 per cent between 7:30 p.m. and 10:30 p.m. While news and public affairs account for about half of the viewing of Canadian programs, Canadian produced entertainment programs only attract 4 per cent of the audience over the total broadcast day.
> French-language Canadian programs account for 62 per cent of the total viewing over the entire day. Canadian produced entertainment shows represent 16 per cent of the programs available and 25 per cent of the viewing time.

In view of the vast amount of incoming foreign (especially U.S.) programs, Canada has been concerned about its cultural values and economic interest since early days of radio broadcasting in Canada. The first Commission on Radio Broadcasting, headed by Sir John Aird in 1929, reported that »the majority of programs heard are from sources outside of Canada.«[221] From the first Canadian Radio Broadcast Act in 1932 to the presently applicable Broadcasting Act of 1968, numerous efforts have been made to control the inflow of foreign broadcasting programs.[222] In addition to a prohibition on deductions from income tax of expenditures incurred for advertising directed at Canadians in foreign television stations, the present regulations regarding the control of foreign programs provide for (a) a requirement of Canadian content in television broadcasting, (b) the retransmitting of a limited number of U.S. television programs via CATV and satellites and (c) the prohibition on the reception of programs transmitted by U.S. satellites.
In 1976 Parliament enacted a law[223] to amend section 19.1 of the Income Tax Act and thereby prohibited a deduction for the expenses of a taxpayer made or incurred after 1976 »for an advertisement directed primarily to a market in Canada and broadcast by a foreign broadcasting undertaking.«[224] »Foreign broadcasting undertaking« for the purpose of this new provision was defined as »a network operation or a broadcasting transmitting undertaking located outside Canada.«[225] The purpose of this new section 19.1 of the Income Tax

220 CRTC Public Notice 1983–18 (1983).
221 CANADIAN ROYAL COMMISSION ON BROADCASTING, REPORT 6 (1929).
222 For details, see D. ELLIS, *supra* note 130; W. EMERY, NATIONAL AND INTERNATIONAL SYSTEMS OF BROADCASTING: THEIR HISTORY, OPERATION AND CONTROL 44 (1969); F. PEERS, *supra* note 130; Gillick, *Public Broadcasting and National Development in Canada*, INTER-MEDIA 18 (Mar. 1985); Mazer, *The Protection of Canadian Culture and the CRTC*, in DECADE OF ADJUSTMENT 97 (J. Menezees ed. 1980).
223 1974–1976 Can. Stat. ch. 106.
224 *Id.* at § 3.
225 *Id.*

Act was to discourage Canadian advertisers from reaching their domestic market via U.S. programs. It was assumed that this action would support the Canadian television production and indirectly minimise the impact of foreign programs. A study of the effect of modified section 19.1 on television advertising showed that it provided a substantial amount of support for the Canadian television industry, as it kept $28 to 33 million from being spent in the U.S. in 1982. »This is equivalent of [sic] 4 or 5 per cent of net private television advertising revenues or 20 to 25 per cent of pre-tax profits in the industry.«[226]

In 1982 the CRTC amended its Television Broadcasting Regulations and promulgated the following provisions with regard to the Canadian-content requirements to be followed by the operators of television broadcasting in Canada:[227]

> [D]uring the 12-month period commencing October 1st in each year, the amount of time devoted by any station or network to the broadcasting of non-Canadian programs shall not,
> (a) between the hours of six o'clock in the forenoon and twelve o'clock midnight, exceed 40 per cent of the total time devoted to broadcasting by that station or network during those hours; or
> (b) between the hours of six o'clock in the afternoon and twelve o'clock midnight
> (i) in case of a station or network for which the Commission has issued a public licence, exceed 40 per cent of the total time devoted to broadcasting by that station or network during those hours; or
> (ii) in the case of a station or network for which the Commission has issued a private licence, exceed 50 per cent of the total time devoted to broadcasting by that station or network during those hours.

Do these regulations violate an individual's rights of freedom of thought, belief, opinion and expression or the right to receive programs? Before the coming into force of the Canadian Charter of Rights and Freedoms, the Supreme Court held in the case of *Re CTV Television Network Ltd. and C.R.T.C.*[228] that the conditions requiring the showing of certain hours of Canadian drama programs imposed on the renewal of a television license were not violative of the right of freedom of speech and that the CRTC was legally entitled to impose such conditions since they are not severable from the

226 Donner & Kliman, *The Effect of Section 19.1 of the Income Tax Act on Television Broadcasting*, 32 CAN. TAX J. 1084, 1095 (1984).
227 CRTC Public Notice 1982–67 (1982).
228 134 D.L.R.3d 193 (Can. 1982).

license. Chief Justice Laskin stated that notwithstanding section 3(c) of the Broadcasting Act, which recognises the right to freedom of expression and an unquestionable right to receive programs, the CRTC could seek »to control or regulate the content programs. ... The Federal Court of Appeal pointed out that no restrictions were imposed on freedom of expression in the drama requirements of the condition and, in my opinion, it was correct in concluding that s.3(c) (even taken at its widest) was not violated.«[229] However, the application of the Charter in a similar case remains to be seen.

The imposition of Canadian content requirements on television broadcasting does not seem to be working effectively to control the inflow of foreign media programs. According to Pierre Juneau, the president of CBC, »Canada and the CBC have discovered that it is impossible to force Canadians to watch Canadian programming, let alone force them to be faithful to their national public broadcaster in an area of overabundance. Culture, like viewing patterns, cannot be legislated or forced.«[230] Therefore, a new approach toward quality programming is advocated,[231] while continuing the previous approach of a quantitative requirement of minimum percentage of Canadian content in broadcasting, though some modifications are also sought.[232]

Under the Cable Television Regulations,[233] the CRTC has allowed the operators of CATV in Canada to carry the signals of only four U.S. television networks – three commercial and one educational (the 3 + 1 rule). This rule also applies to Canadian Satellite Communications, Inc. (CanCom), which provides service via satellite to CATV operators in the northern areas of Canada.[234] It may be restated here that the CRTC has the power to allow CATV operators to remove commercials from incoming U.S. television signals and replace them with their own.[235] This power can be used not only to

229 *Id.* at 200.

230 Juneau, *Audience Fragmentation and Cultural Erosion: A Canadian Perspective on Challenge for the Public Broadcaster*, 35(2) EBU REVIEW 14 (1984). Mr. Juneau's views are the result of continued difficulties faced by the government in the imposition of minimum Canadian content requirements on broadcasters who could never meet these requirements because of economic realities. In other words, Canadian broadcasters are able to purchase programs of superior quality from U.S. producers at a fraction of what it would cost them to produce similar programs in Canada. A further incentive for Canadian broadcasters to purchase popular U.S. programs is the far greater advertising revenues that they generate, as compared with Canadian productions. *See* Policy Statement on Canadian Content in Television, *supra* note 220.

231 DEPARTMENT OF COMMUNICATIONS, NATIONAL FILM AND VIDEO POLICY (1984).

232 *See* CRTC, PROPOSED CRITERIA: RECOGNITION OF CANADIAN PROGRAMS (Public Notice 1984–56) (1984).

233 1975 CAN. STAT. O. & REGS. 665, *as amended by* CRTC Public Notice 1981–97 (1981).

234 For details, see CRTC, PROCEDURES RELATED TO THE IMPLEMENTATION OF THE »3 + 1« CANCOM SERVICES (Public Notice 1983–114) (1983); *Canada Firm Uses Scrambled TV Signal, Decoder*, Aviation Week and Space Technology, Jan. 7, 1984, at 103.

235 *See* CRTC Public Announcement, *supra* note 206.

control the inflow of U.S. television programs but also to increase the financial capability of the Canadian CATV operators.

The CRTC may legally impose conditions on licenses of CATV operators, prohibiting them from receiving and retransmitting certain U.S. programs transmitted by satellites whose signals spill over in Canada. The Supreme Court of Newfoundland (Court of Appeal) in the case of *R. v. Shellbird Cable Ltd.*,[236] in reversing the decision of the lower court, held that the CRTC had the power under section 16 of the Broadcasting Act to make regulations prohibiting the interception and distribution of the signals of U.S. satellites.

On the other hand, the reception by individuals in Canada of U.S. programs transmitted by satellites cannot be prohibited by the CRTC. According to the government, television signals transmitted by U.S. satellites operating with radio frequencies allocated to the Fixed-Satellite Service were private signals; thus, the approval of the signal originator was required before they could be intercepted in Canada.[237] However, the Federal Court (Trial Division) in *Lount Corporation v. A.G. Canada*[238] held that television signals transmitted by U.S. satellites (in the Fixed-Satellite Service) were in fact broadcast signals and thus legally receivable by the general public in Canada. Moreover, Justice Muldoon stated that »subject only to the provisions of the [Broadcasting] Act and Regulations, the unquestioned right of persons to receive programs must be understood to be an unlimited, unfettered, unregulated or unrestricted right, since Parliament characterised it as unquestioned.« Therefore, this unquestioned right entitles individuals and entities that are not broadcasting receiving undertakings to receive TV programs transmitted by U.S. satellites.

4. *Legal Relationship Between Media Companies and Individuals*

Audiovisual media establish a close relationship between the media companies (the providers of information) and the individuals or the public (the receivers and sometimes the subjects of information). This relationship is governed by certain legally recognised rights and duties shared by both sides of the

236 108 Atl. Prov. 224 (Nfld. C.A. 1982), 38 Nfld. & P.E.I. 224 (1982).

237 *Fox Announces Publication of New Earth Station Regulations*, Department of Communications News Release, May 17, 1983.

238 [1984] 1 F.C. 332, 362 (F.C.T.D.).

relationship. We shall discuss here some of the important areas in which there is a likelihood that the rights of the one side might be violated by the other side during the process of gathering, disseminating and receiving information – the essential activities of the audiovisual media.

a) *Protection of Privacy*

In four provinces, invasion of an individual's privacy is protected under statutory laws, while in others, common-law remedies are available to individuals.

Article 1053 of the Quebec Civil Code has been invoked to protect an individual's privacy, providing that »[e]very person capable of discerning right from wrong is responsible for the damage by his fault, of another, whether by positive act, imprudence, neglect or want of care.« During the early years of television, this article was interpreted to provide protection against the violation of an individual's privacy. In the case of *Robbins v. CBC*,[239] the plaintiff, a Montreal doctor who had written a critical letter to a popular CBC television show originating in Toronto, became a victim of hostile letters and phone calls after the host of the program announced his name and address and suggested that the viewers should »cheer him up.« Because of such calls and letters, he had to change his phone number and suffered loss in his medical practice. The Supreme Court of Quebec held the defendant CBC liable for damages for invasion of the plaintiff's privacy under article 1053.

Since 1968 British Columbia, Saskatchewan and Manitoba have also passed protection of privacy acts.[240] Exept for minor details, they are essentially similar. Section 2 of the Manitoba Privacy Act, for example, states that »[a] person who substantially, unreasonably and without claim of right, violates the privacy of another person, commits a tort against that person.« For suing the accused, there is no need of proving any actual damage to the plaintiff. Section 3(a) of the Act provides that a violation will occur when a person is put under surveillance through the use of a camera directed at that person's home or other place of residence. The Act, however, specifies various defences.[241]

In other provinces, where protection of privacy acts are not to be found, common-law remedies are available, mainly in the form of protection against

239 12 D.L.R.2d 35 (Que. Sup. Ct. 1958).

240 Privacy Act, B.C. REV. STAT. ch. 336 (1979), *as amended by* 1982 B.C. Stat. ch. 46; Privacy Act, SASK. REV. STAT. ch. P–24 (1978); Privacy Act, 1970 Man. Stat. ch. 74.

241 1970 Man. Stat. ch. 74, § 5.

defamation, slander and libel.[242] It may be noted that, at common law, invasion of privacy per se is not an offence, but the common law provides remedies through laws pertaining to defamation or protection of honor.[243]

b) *Illicit Advertising*

As noted earlier,[244] the Television Broadcasting Regulations prohibit television stations from advertising any thing or act prohibited by law, e.g., prostitution services. Advertisement using a person's endorsement without his permission is also prohibited. In *Athans v. Canadian Adventure Camps Ltd.*,[245] the defendant, who used a photograph of the plaintiff without his consent for commercial promotion purposes, was held liable for damages for misappropriation of the personality of the plaintiff.
The Manitoba Privacy Act replaces this common-law action of misappropriation of personality, stating that the privacy of a person may be violated:

> by the unauthorised use of the name or likeness or voice of that person for the purpose of advertising or promoting the sale of, or any other trading in any property or services, or for any other purpose of gain to the user if, in the course of the use, that person is identified or identifiable and the user intended to exploit the name or likeness or voice of that person.[246]

Thus, in Canada both common law and statutory law are sufficiently clear with respect to illicit advertising.

c) *Protection of Copyright*

Copyright law prohibits the copying of an original work without the consent of the holder of the copyright. The law is based on the premise that exclusive rights regarding the reproduction of a work belong to the copyright holder, who will lose his incentive to create if he loses these rights. Copyright however

242 For details, see Gibson, *Legal Protection of Privacy*, in THE PRACTICE OF FREEDOM: CANADIAN ESSAYS ON HUMAN RIGHTS AND FUNDAMENTAL FREEDOMS 179 (1979); C. BECKTON, *supra* note 172, at 128.
243 Gibson, *supra* note 242; C. BECKTON, *supra* note 172.
244 *See supra* pp. 77–78.
245 4 C.C.L.T. 20 (Ont. H.C. 1978). *See also* Krouse v. Chrysler Canada, 40 D.L.R.3d 15 (Ont. C.A. 1974).
246 1970 Man. Stat. ch. 74, § 3(c).

is not an absolute right. The holder of this right may not be allowed to enforce it if publication or multiplication of his work is desirable in the public interest.

To provide reciprocal copyright protection to the copyright holders of other nations, international conventions have been devised. There are two main international copyright conventions: the Berne Convention of 1886[247] and the Universal Copyright Convention (UCC) of 1952.[248] Since Canada, a party to both Conventions, has its most important audiovisual media relations with the U.S., which is party only to the UCC,[249] it is logical to discuss the UCC in this context. Under article I, states parties to the UCC have undertaken to provide »adequate and effective protection« for the rights of authors and other copyright holders. The UCC neither expressly provides protection to the broadcasters nor excludes such protection. According to article V(1), »[c]opyright shall include the exclusive right of the author to make, publish and authorize the making and publication of translations of works protected under the Convention.«

However, article VI defines »publication« very restrictively: »›Publication‹, as used in this Convention, means the reproduction in tangible form and the general distribution to the public of the copies of a work from which it can be read or otherwise visually perceived.« The definition does not appear to cover the broadcasting of film or other programs, though it includes the making of a film. Therefore, the Convention does not provide protection for a U.S. broadcaster or producer of programs that are available »on the air« in Canada and can be intercepted legally without violation of any obligation under the UCC.

Moreover, the Convention requires »national treatment«; that is, the protection of American copyright must stem from Canadian law. The exact meaning of »adequate and effective protection« under article I is to be decided by the national law of a state party to the Convention. Canada provides such protection under its Copyright Act.[250] It does not infringe its international obligations under the UCC even though the protection provided by the Act may be inadequate and ineffective according to the laws of other states parties to the Convention.

247 Convention for the Creation of an International Union for the Protection of Literary and Artistic Works, Sept. 9, 1886, 168 Consol. T.S. 185. The Convention has gone through various revisions by protocols of Berlin (1908), Berne (1914), Rome (1928), Brussels (1948), Stockholm (1967) and Paris (1971). The U.S. is not a party to this Convention.

248 Sept. 6, 1952, 216 U.N.T.S. 134. It has been in force for Canada since Aug. 10, 1962.

249 1980 TREATIES IN FORCE 272 and Appendix.

250 CAN. REV. STAT. ch. C-30 (1970).

The Copyright Act came into force on January 1, 1924 and has remained almost unchanged, despite tremendous technological innovations in the audiovisual media. Section 3(1) of the Act provides a specific definition of copyright:

> For the purposes of this Act, ›Copyright‹ means the sole right to produce or reproduce the work or any substantial part thereof in any material form whatever, to perform, or in the case of a lecture to deliver, the work or any substantial part thereof in public; if the work is unpublished, to publish the work or any substantial part thereof; and includes the sole right:
>
> (a) to produce, reproduce, perform or publish any translation of the work;
> (b) in the case of a dramatic work, to convert it into a novel or other nondramatic work;
> (c) in the case of a novel or other non-dramatic work, or of an artistic work, to convert it into a dramatic work, by way of performance in public or otherwise;
> (d) in the case of literary, dramatic or musical work, to make any record, perforated roll, cinematograph film, or other contrivance by means of which the work may be mechanically performed or delivered;
> (e) in the case of any literary, dramatic, musical or artistic work, to reproduce, adapt and publicly present such work by cinematographic, if the author has given such work an original character;
> (f) in the case of any literary, dramatic, musical or artistic work, to communicate such work by radio communication;
>
> and to authorise such acts as aforesaid.

Original literary, dramatic, musical and artistic works are protected if their copyright holders are Canadian citizens, British subjects or residents within Her Majesty's Dominion, or citizens or subjects of foreign coutries that are parties to the copyright conventions ratified by Canada. As far as audiovisual media is concerned, the terms »work« and »perform« as used in section 3 are important. »Work,« within the meaning of the Act, must be expressed in a form of identification. Performance is defined as any presentation, including that »by radio communication.«[251]

To clarify these terms, the case of *Canadian Admiral Corp. Ltd. v. Rediffusion Inc.*[252] is important. In this case, the defendant intercepted the plaintiff's live broadcast signals and retransmitted them via cable to his subscribers. It was held that a live broadcast was incapable of copyright protection as there was no originality in the work; thus, the signals were not a »work« within the meaning of section 3 of the Copyright Act. It was also held

251 *Id.* at § 2.
252 20 Can. Pat. 75 (Exch. 1954), 1954 Can. Exch. 382.

that the transmission via cable was not »radio communication«; thus, a CATV operator does not infringe copyright. Moreover, the transmission of the program to private home television sets was held not to be a »performance« within the meaning of the Copyright Act, which requires that a performance be in »public.« Exchequer Court Judge Cameron did not accept that »even a large number of private performances, solely because of their numbers, can become public performances.«[253]

In the later case of *Composers, Authors and Publishers Association of Canada (CAPAC) v. CTV Television Network*,[254] the Supreme Court reached a conclusion similar to the one in the *Canadian Admiral* case. In the *CAPAC* case, the plaintiff tried to obtain a fee from the CTV network, which was for distributing copyrighted work of CAPAC via the microwave facilities of Bell Canada to its affiliates for further transmission to the public. The Court unanimously held that the cable or microwave transmission by the network to its affiliates is not a performance in public of the work of the copyright holders.

In light of these decisions, transmissions of U.S. television programs by CanCom (a Canadian satellite transmission company) to its affiliate CATV operators in the northern areas are not performances in public and thus do not violate the copyright of the U.S. performers, authors or broadcasting companies, as the case may be.[255]

In Canada, the concept of »fair use« is given a narrow construction, and »most home video recording would not constitute fair dealing and would be regarded, therefore, as infringement.«[256] Similarly, the recording and transmission by a CATV operator of a copyright program is an infringement of copyright under the Copyright Act. According to Judge Cattanch in *Warner Bros. Seven Arts Inc. v. CESM-TV Ltd.*,[257] material contained in broadcasts may be protected by copyright, but the protection attaches only to that material and not to the broadcast itself. Therefore, the video recording of television programs by a CATV system for retransmission, as happened in this case, constitutes unauthorised replication by a »contrivance by means of which the work may be mechanically performed,« as specified in section 3(1) of the Copyright Act.[258]

253 1954 Can. Exch. at 408.
254 68 D.L.R.2d 98 (Can. 1968).
255 For details, see Tarbet, *Use of American Broadcast Signals by Canadian Cable Networks: The CanCom Decision*, 32 BUFFALO L. REV. 731 (1983).
256 Van Dyck, *Fast-Forward: A Canadian Perspective on the Betamax Controversy*, 16 OTTAWA L. REV. 506, 518 (1984).
257 65 Can. Pat. 215 (1971).
258 *Id.* at 241.

Copyright in radiowaves or signals per se cannot be maintained in Canada. This view, expressed in the *Warner Bros.* case, was further supported by Judge Thurlow of the Federal Court of Appeal in *Capital Cities Communications Inc. v. Canadian Radio-Television Commission.*[259] He stated:

> The appellants have no proprietary or other legal rights in their signals in Canadian air space. The radio frequencies in that space are public property under section 3(a) of the *Broadcasting Act*. When the appellants put out signals on any or such frequencies, they make use of the public property in the frequencies but they do not by so doing acquire any right either in the frequency or the signals they have generated on it, and they have no right to have their signals received in Canada in any form, whether altered or unaltered.

The Court of Appeal affirmed the power of the CRTC to order or permit the deletion of advertising messages contained in broadcasts that originate in the U.S. and are distributed in Canada by CATV operators. This judgment was upheld by the Supreme Court.[260]

In copyright cases involving conflict-of-law questions, it is Canadian law that applies if the infringement takes place in Canada (i.e., if the programs are received in Canada), irrespective of the fact that the copyright program originates from outside Canada. In the case of *CAPAC v. International Good Music Inc.*,[261] the defendant broadcast certain musical works having Canadian copyright into Canada from the U.S. The Supreme Court, applying *Jenner v. Sun Oil Co.*,[262] held the defendant liable for infringement of copyright under the Copyright Act, stating:

> [I]t seems arguable that a person who has held himself out to advertisers as being able to communicate, by means of his American television transmitter, with some million persons in British Columbia, if he transmits musical works, of which the appellant has the Canadian copyright, to viewers in Canada who receive such programs, has thereby communicated in Canada such musical works by radio communication within the provisions of the Copyright Act.[263]

It can be concluded that in Canada: CATV operators bear no legal liability for the retransmission in Canada of copyrighted U.S. broadcast programs; home video recording of »on-the-air« programs and video recording for the purpose of retransmission constitute an infringement of copyright; it is the contents of

259 1975 F.C. 18, 20, 52 D.L.R.3d 415, 417 (Fed. C.A. 1974).
260 *Capital Cities*, [1978] 2 S.C.R. 141.
261 1963 S.C.R. 136.
262 1952 Ont. 240 (H.C.).
263 1963 S.C.R. at 144.

a program, not the signals per se, that are entitled to copyright; and the Canadian law of copyright will be applicable if infringement of that right occurs in Canada. As important exporters of audiovisual programs to Canada and having no legal remedy for the infringement of their copyrighted programs, U.S. broadcasters have been pressing for payments from Canadian CATV operators, through courts and politics. They view this situation as an imbalance of copyright protection since »U.S. law assures Canadian program producers of payment for use of their copyrighted material, but Canadian law does not require the payment of royalties to American copyright owners.«[264] The Canadian government is not unaware of the problem.[265] However, it does not presently seem to be keen on the revision of sixty-years-old legislation, despite strong recommendations emerging from a specialised and extensive study of copyright issues in Canada.[266] However, since 1983 Canada has levied an 8% tax on CATV operators,[267] though the distribution of the collected funds has not been yet clarified.

264 *Copyright Office Seeks to Stem Foreign Losses*, Broadcasting, Oct. 8, 1984, at 81.

265 M. Masse, Copyright Revision: Towards a New Era (statement by the Minister of Communications to the Sub-Committee on Communication and Culture on the Revision of Copyright), *reprinted in* Communications, May 9, 1985.

266 A. KEYES & C. BRUNET, COPYRIGHT IN CANADA: PROPOSALS FOR A REVISION OF THE LAW (1977).

267 From notes for a speech by Francis Fox to the Canadian Association of Broadcasters, Oct. 26, 1983.

Chapter VII: Establishment of Foreign Program Companies and Transmitting Companies in Canada.

A. *Foreign Program Companies*

The establishment of foreign program companies in Canada as business enterprises is regulated by the relevant municipal, provincial and federal laws, which are too numerous to be discussed here. However, the Foreign Investment Review Act of 1973,[268] the most important federal law relating to establishment and acquisition of business enterprises, including program companies, deserves discussion. The Act implements the policy of economic protectionism advocated by the Watkins Report[269] and establishes a procedure for the systematic review of proposals for the establishment or acquisition of businesses of all kinds in Canada by foreigners. Since foreign investment is a matter of »national concern«[270] to Canada, the review of such proposals is carried out by the highest political decision-making body in Canada: the Governor-in-Council.

According to section 8 of the Act, every non-eligible person and every group of persons, any member of which is a non-eligible person, that proposes to acquire control of a Canadian business enterprise or to establish a new business in Canada is required to give notice in writing to the Foreign Investment Review Agency, established under the Act, in such form and manner and containing such information as is prescribed by the regulations[271] promulgated under section 28 of the Act.

Section 3(1) of the Act provides an exhaustive definition of the term »non-eligible person.« The term means (a) an individual who is neither a Canadian citizen nor a permanent resident (landed immigrant) of Canada, (b) the government or a political subdivision of a foreign country, or (c) a corporation incorporated in Canada or elsewhere that is controlled by foreigners.

268 1973–1974 Can. Stat. ch. 46, *as amended by* 1974–1976 Can. Stat. ch. 52 and 1980–1983 Can. Stat. ch. 107.

269 TASK FORCE ON THE STRUCTURE OF CANADIAN INDUSTRY, REPORT: FOREIGN OWNERSHIP AND THE STRUCTURE OF THE CANADIAN INDUSTRY (1968). The Task Force was headed by M. Melville Watkins.

270 1973–1974 Can. Stat. ch. 46, § 2.

271 Regulations Respecting the Acquisition of Control of Canadian Business Enterprises and the Establishment of New Businesses in Canada, 1983 CAN. STAT. O. & REGS. 493.

If the Minister responsible for the administration of the Act has reasonable and probable grounds to believe that a person or group of persons has not given notice to the Agency as required under section 8, he may require that person or group to give such notice.[272] The Agency, which, in fact, is a subdivision of an ordinary department of the federal government, is responsible for advising and assisting the Minister. After notice under section 8 is received by the Agency, it is referred to the Minister. He, in turn, reviews the information contained in the notice, as well as other information submitted by third parties, for the purpose of assessing whether the investment is going to be of significant benefit to Canada.

»Significant benefit« is determined by taking into consideration various factors enumerated in section 2(2) of the Act. These factors are quite general in nature and thus allow the Minister great discretion. According to Langford, »every different factor in different applications will tend to vary the result of each.«[273]

The Minister sends his findings on »significant benefit« and his recommendations to the Governor-in-Council, which makes the final decision regarding the allowance of the proposed foreign investment.[274] The final decision must be communicated through the Agency to the original proposer within sixty days of the receipt of notice by the Agency; otherwise there is presumption that the Governor-in-Council has allowed the investment.[275] Willful noncompliance with the review process under the Act has been declared an offence punishable by a fine not exceeding 5000 dollars.[276]

It is generally recognised that Canada needs and gains much from foreign investment; thus nearly 95% of the review applications in 1983 for the acquisition of Canadian businesses or the establishment of new businesses in Canada were allowed.[277] However, the Act, from its inception, has been very unpopular with the foreign investment community and has been viewed as a major deterrent to foreign investment in Canada. Therefore, the present Progressive-Conservative federal government has planned to replace the Act's foreign investment review regime with the »Investment Canada« regime proposed under Bill C-15, »An Act Respecting Investment in Canada.«[278]

272 1973–1974 Can. Stat. ch. 46, § 8(3).

273 J. LANGFORD, CANADIAN FOREIGN INVESTMENT CONTROLS 74 (3d. ed. 1983).

274 1973–1974 Can. Stat. ch. 46, § 12.

275 *Id.* at § 13.

276 *Id.* at § 24.

277 J. LANGFORD, *supra* note 273, at 75.

278 Bill C–15, 33d Parliament, 33 & 34 Eliz. 2 (1984–1985) (as passed by the House of Commons on June 6, 1985).

Though the Bill has been adopted by the House of Commons, it has not yet become law in Canada.
The purpose of Bill C-15 is to encourage investment in Canada – by Canadians and non-Canadians alike – that contributes to Canadian economic growth and employment opportunities; the Bill provides for continued review of significant investments in Canada by non-Canadians in order to ensure such benefit to Canada. The administrative agency proposed under the Bill is the »Investment Canada Agency,« whose main functions would be to advise and assist the federal Minister in encouraging foreign investment in Canada and to review certain foreign-investment proposals. While the overall thrust of the new legislation is to encourage foreign investment, section 16(1) of the Bill provides that »[a] non-Canadian shall not implement an investment reviewable under this Act unless the investment has been reviewed under this Act and the Minister is satisfied or is deemed to be satisfied that the investment is likely to be of net benefit to Canada.«
»Net benefit« is less rigorous than the »significant benefit« standard under the present Foreign Investment Review Act. This distinction, in addition to the absence of the »national concern« factor, seems to convey a signal generally favourable to foreign investment.
Section 20 of Bill C-15 enumerates various factors that must be taken into consideration in assessing whether a foreign investment proposal is likely to be of net benefit to Canada. These factors are similar to those mentioned in section 2 of the present Act, except the one enumeratred in section 20(e):

> The compatibility of the investment with national industrial, economic and cultural policies, taking into consideration industrial, economic and cultural policy objectives enunciated by the government or legislature of any province likely to be significantly affected by the investment.

Moreover, section 15 of the Bill contains a reserve power for the review of investment in »culturally sensitive industries«:

> An investment subject to notification under Part III that would not otherwise be reviewable is reviewable under this Part if
> (a) it falls within a prescribed specific type of business activity that, in the opinion of the Governor in Council, is related to Canada's cultural heritage or national identity; ...

In view of (1) the special consideration given »cultural policies« in reviewing foreign investment proposals and (2) foreign investment, otherwise unreviewable, being made reviewable because of its affinity to »Canada's cultural heritage or national identity,« it seems that economic activities of publishing and media industries have been given express considerations not found under the present Act. It is, at present, difficult to speculate whether this move will discourage or encourage foreign investment in the Canadian television programming industry, especially since the federal government has not clearly established its »cultural policy« and Bill C-15 is not yet law.

B. *Foreign Transmitting Companies*

The law on the establishment of audiovisual media transmitting companies in Canada clearly stems from section 3(b) of the Broadcasting Act,[279] which states that »the Canadian broadcasting system should be effectively owned and controlled by Canadians.«

> Before 1968, Parliament and the regulatory authority had allowed a number of stations to come under the ownership or control of companies from Great Britain or the United States (for example, Paramount Pictures and PKO-General Tire and Rubber). In cable television, by 1967 United States companies owned or controlled the services used by 77 per cent of all Canadian subscribers – approximately twenty of these systems were owned substantially by the subsidiaries of CBS and of Gulf and Western Industries.[280]

However, the Broadcasting Act changed that situation. In 1969, under section 27 of the Act, the Governor-in-Council issued a directive[281] to the CRTC that it not issue a broadcasting license to a non-Canadian and that it not renew, if already issued, the license of any such person. This directive was replaced by two other directives[282] in 1971 and 1972, which presently prohibit the CRTC from issuing any broadcasting licenses under the Broadcasting Act to the following:

(a) persons who are not Canadian citizens or eligible Canadian corporations;
(b) governments of countries other than Canada or of political subdivisions of countries other than Canada and agents of such governments; and

279 CAN. REV. STAT. ch. B–11 (1970).
280 Peers, *supra* note 120, at 79.
281 1969 CAN. STAT. O. & REGS. 590.
282 CAN. CONSOL. REG. chs. 376–77 (1978).

(c) Her Majesty in right of any province of Canada, and agents of Her Majesty in right of any province.

For the purpose of these directives, an »eligible Canadian corporation« is a corporation:

(a) that is incorporated under the laws of Canada or a province;
(b) of which the chairman or other presiding officer and each of the directors or other similar officers are Canadian citizens; and
(c) of which, if it is a corporation having share capital, at least four-fifths of the shares having full voting rights are beneficially owned by Canadian citizens.

In brief, foreigners are allowed a share participation of only 20 percent in any broadcasting, including audiovisual media, company in Canada.

Chapter VIII: Regulation of the Flow of Media Programs Out of Canada.

Law and regulations governing the flow of media programs from abroad to Canada, as discussed above,[283] is of direct relevance and application to the flow of media programs from Canada to abroad. Hence, they need not be repeated here. However, a discussion of the process of regulation and other related issues regarding the Canadian audiovisual media seems necessary and important.

A. *International Law*

Canadian television transmissions within 250 miles of the U.S.-Canada border are carried out in accordance with the 1952 U.S.-Canada TV bilateral agreement.[284] Any future DBS service must not be directed at the territory of the U.S. or any other country, beyond the area of technically unavoidable spillover, unless there is an agreement between Canada and the receiving state. This prohibition, incorporated in paragraph No. 2674 of the ITU Radio Regulations, and the provisions of the 1952 U.S.-Canada TV bilateral agreement must be followed by Canadian DBS operators.[285] While we have discussed[286] the human rights conventions applicable in Canada to the audiovisual media, it may be added that any restriction on the ownership of broadcasting systems or on the requirement of a minimum Canadian content in programs is not considered to be in conflict with article 19 of the International Covenant on Civil and Political Rights.[287]

According to the *Report of Canada* on the implementations of the Covenant,

> [t]hese policies are not, in fact, intended to restrict freedom of expression, but rather to ensure the development of a Canadian broadcasting system and to protect

283 *See supra* pp. 62–96.
284 Agreement, *supra* note 142.
285 *See supra* note 145 and accompanying text.
286 *See supra* pp. 65–69.
287 *Supra* note 161, at 85.

> and enrich Canadian culture and strengthen the political, social and economic structure of the country. In other words, these restrictions, which pertain to the administration of the public domain, are justified on the grounds of public policy.[288]

Moreover, in Canada the fundamental right of freedom of expression has been recognised in section 2(b) of the Canadian Charter of Rights and Freedoms, as well as in section 3(c) of the Broadcasting Act.

B. *National Law*

The Department of Communications Act[289] specifies the duties, powers and functions of the Federal Minister of Communications for all matters that come within the jurisdiction of Parliament. However, his more specific authority over audiovisual media comes from the Radio Act[290] and the Broadcasting Act.[291]
Section 3(1) of the Radio Act states that:

> [N]o person shall
> a) establish a radio station, or install, operate or have in his possession a radio apparatus at any place in Canada or on board any
>
> ....
>
> (e) spacecraft under the direction or control of Her Majesty in right of Canada or a province, a citizen or resident of Canada or a Corporation incorporated or resident in Canada, except under and in accordance with a licence and, to the extent that it is a broadcasting undertaking, except under and in accordance with a technical construction and operating certificate, issued by the Minister under this Act.

»Radio station« is defined as a place in which a radio apparatus is located, and radio apparatus means a reasonably complete and sufficient combination of distinct appliances intended for or capable of being used for radiocommunication.[292] Under section 6(1) of the Radio Act, the Governor-in-Council has the authority to determine to whom licenses may be issued; this, in turn,

288 *Id.* at 85–86.
289 CAN. REV. STAT. ch. C–24, *as amended* (1970).
290 CAN. REV. STAT. ch. R–1 (1970).
291 CAN. REV. STAT. ch. B–11 (1970).
292 CAN. REV. STAT. ch. R–1, § 2(1) (1970).

determines who may operate broadcasting systems, including DBS. Although, at present, satellite telecommunications have been monopolised by Telesat Canada,[293] a public corporation jointly owned by the federal government and major common carriers, private ownership of spacecraft, consequently DBS, is allowed under the above-mentioned section 3(1) of the Radio Act.

The Minister of Communications may prescribe classes of licenses and of technical construction and operating certificates.[294] Such certificates are issued in respect of radio stations and radio apparatuses to the extent that they are broadcasting undertakings.[295] The Minister's authority over broadcasting is established under section 5 of the Radio Act, which requires him to »regulate and control all technical matters relating to the planning for and the construction and operation of broadcasting facilities.« »Broadcasting undertaking« is defined in the Radio Act as well as the Broadcasting Act to include broadcasting transmitting undertakings and broadcasting receiving undertakings;[296] in other words, the term covers radio, TV, CATV and DBS. The Minister enjoys wide discretion in the issuance of technical construction and operating certificates and may impose upon them such terms and conditions as he considers appropriate.[297] He may amend such conditions where he considers such amendment necessary for the purpose for which the original conditions were provided.[298] He may also suspend or revoke any certificate where he is satisfied that the holder of the certificate has willfully failed to operate the radio station in accordance with the regulations or the conditions of his certificate or that the certificate was obtained by fraud.[299] »The scope of his discretion is so great that in the case where technical construction and operating certificate is issued this wide discretion could be used to usurp the licensing authority of the CRTC over broadcasting.«[300] However, any suspension or revocation of a technical construction and operation certificate must either be with the consent of the holder thereof or, in any other case, when notice of intention to suspend or revoke the certificate has been given to the holder and he has also been given a reasonable opportunity to be heard.[301]

293 *See* Telesat Canada Act, CAN. REV. STAT. ch. T–4 (1970).
294 CAN. REV. STAT. ch. R–1, § 4(1)(a) (1970).
295 *Id.* at § 4(1)(b)(ii).
296 *Id.* at § 2(1); Broadcasting Act, CAN. REV. STAT. ch. B–11 (1970).
297 Radio Act, CAN. REV. STAT. ch. R–1, § 4(1)(b) (1970).
298 *Id.* at § 4(1)(c).
299 *Id.* at § 4(1)(d).
300 Cooper, *supra* note 135, at 111.
301 Radio Act, CAN. REV. STAT. ch. R–1, § 4(2) (1970).

The Minister has the authority to make regulations with respect to (a) the use of radio frequencies, the power employed and the nature of the broadcasting service to be rendered,[302] as well as (b) the form and manner of applications for a technical construction and operating certificate.[303] Neither the Radio Act, nor the General Radio Regulations[304] promulgated pursuant to the Act, contain any provision for a formal hearing of the application for a technical construction and operating certificate for a broadcasting undertaking. Nor do they provide for any judicial review of the decisions of the Minister in case of a refusal of the application or a suspension and revocation of the certificate.
Section 3(3) of the Radio Act exempts certain radio stations or apparatuses from the requirement of a license under section 3(1). It states that:

> Any radio station or radio apparatus that is capable only of receiving radiocommunications and that is not a broadcasting receiving undertaking is exempt from the requirements of subsection (1) if it is intended only for the reception of
> (a) broadcasting; or
> (b) broadcasting and any class of radiocommunication, other than broadcasting, prescribed by the Minister.

Thus, television sets in general use are exempt from the requirement of a license. However, with respect to the TVRO (TV Receive-Only) earth stations (antennae) that receive radiocommunications from satellites, the government has adopted a different policy: it restricted the licensing of TVROs to broadcasters, common carriers and CATV operators.[305] With the extensive decrease in the cost of TVROs, their number has rapidly increased, especially for individual home units. Therefore, the government, pursuant to section 7(3) of the Radio Act, adopted new regulations exempting TVROs for private individuals from the requirement of a license.[306] In addition to private individuals, commercial establishments, such as bars and nightclubs, are also exempted from the TVRO regulations, provided the signals received are not redistributed to others.[307]
However, according to a 1983 policy statement by the federal government:

302 *Id.* at §§ 5(b), 7(1)(b).
303 *Id.* at § 4(a).
304 CAN. CONSOL. REG. chs. 1371–72 (1978).
305 Department of Communications News Release, Nov. 24, 1980.
306 General Radio Regulations, Part II, Amendment, 1983 CAN. STAT. O. & REGS. 422. The present Progressive-Conservative government has carried over this policy of exempting the TVROs of private individuals from the requirement of a license. *See* Department of Communications News Release, Dec. 20, 1984.
307 News Release, *supra* note 306.

> Condominiums, apartment buildings, hotels, motels and other multi-unit buildings that receive and distribute local radio and television programming signals via their own cable systems (known as master antenna TV or MATV systems), are classified as broadcasting receiving undertakings and must also apply to the CRTC for authority to receive and distribute radio and television signals transmitted by satellite. Where permission is granted by the CRTC under such conditions, a radio licence will not be required under the Radio Act.[308]

This policy liberalized the reception by private individuals of television signals from Canadian satellites only and not those from U.S. satellites. Similarly, a 1984 policy statement prohibited the reception of satellite television signals transmitted by U.S. satellites and specified that

> [s]atellite master antenna television (SMATV) systems, such as those used by some hotels, apartment buildings and condominiums, will continue to be exempt from licensing as long as they offer those services authorised for delivery by the cable operator in the area.[309]

However, the decision in the *Lount Corporation*[310] case has overruled this policy, at least as far as the reception of satellite TV signals (including those from U.S. satellites) by hotels is concerned. In that case, the lower court held that Canadian law does not vest the government or its agencies with the power needed to implement their current policies on TVROs. The court indicated, however, that this lacuna can be filled by amending legislation by Parliament but not merely by regulations made pursuant to the present Broadcasting Act and the Radio Act.

The Canadian Radio-television and Telecommunications Commission Act[311] established the CRTC and, in section 14, provided it with powers with respect to broadcasting. The Broadcasting Act specifies the objectives of the CRTC. Except on technical matters, the CRTC enjoys comprehensive regulatory[312] and supervisory (including licensing[313]) powers relating to all aspects of Canadian broadcasting (including audiovisual media); this enables the CRTC to achieve the above-mentioned objectives and to implement the broadcasting policy declared in section 3 of the Broadcasting Act.

The CRTC may make regulations in various specified areas relating to broadcasting as well as »respecting such other matters as it deems necessary

308 Department of Communications News Release, May 17, 1983 (NR 83–39).
309 News Release, *supra* note 306.
310 [1984] 1 F.C. 332 (F.C.T.D.).
311 1974–1976 Can. Stat. ch. 49.
312 CAN. REV. STAT. ch. B–11, § 16 (1970).
313 *Id.* at § 17.

for the furtherance of its objectives.«[314] In furtherance thereof, the CRTC may prescribe classes of licenses, issue licenses and revoke them.[315]
No broadcasting undertaking (including TV, CATV and DBS) can be carried on without a valid license from the CRTC. The CRTC may issue licenses for terms not exceeding five years and may impose such conditions as it deems appropriate for the implementation of the broadcasting policy.[316] In connection with an application for the issuance of a broadcast license, the CRTC must hold public hearings,[317] although it has the discretion to decide whether such hearings are necessary.[318] The CRTC Rules of Procedure[319] prescribe detailed procedures to be followed for the issuance, amendment and renewal of broadcast licenses. The character of the broadcast hearings is informal.
Through its power to place conditions of broadcast licenses, the CRTC effectively wields policy-making power, which has, in fact, increased the regulatory and supervisory functions of the CRTC to a significant extent. It is through this power that the CRTC regulates service tariffs charged by CATV operators. Even though the TV signals – from both Canadian and U.S. television stations – are »on the air« and available to the public free of charge, a CATV operator is allowed to charge a service fee, the maximum amount of which is included as a condition in his license. In order to increase rates, a CATV operator must apply for an amendment to his license. All conditions attached to broadcast licenses have the force of law and thus are appealable to the Federal Court.[320] The CRTC, therefore, has elevated its policy statements to the status of regulations without promulgating actual regulations, and this power has been upheld by the courts.[321]
The decisions of the CRTC on applications for broadcast licenses are final, except in two cases. Upon the leave of the court, an appeal lies with the Federal Court of Appeal on a question of law and jurisdiction.[322] An application for leave of the court must be filed within one month after the making of the decision from which an appeal is sought. An appeal must be laid within sixty days from the day leave has been obtained.[323] CRTC

314 *Id.* at § 16(1)(b).
315 *Id.* at §§ 16(1)(a), 17(1), 16(1)(c).
316 *Id.* at § 17(1)(a).
317 *Id.* at § 19(1).
318 National Indian Brotherhood v. Juneau, 1971 F.C. 498 (F.C.T.D.) (affirming such discretionary powers of the CRTC).
319 CAN. CONSOL. REG. ch. 375 (1978).
320 *See* R. BABE, *supra* note 130, at 37.
321 *Capital Cities*, [1978] 2 S.C.R. 141.
322 Broadcasting Act, CAN. REV. STAT. ch. B–11, § 26 (1970).
323 *Id.* at § 26(2).

decisions are also reviewable by the Governor-in-Council within sixty days of such decisions.[324] As a consequence of this, the decisions of the CRTC with respect to the issuance, amendment or renewal of broadcast licenses may be set aside or may be referred back to the CRTC for reconsideration. This reviewing power of the Governor-in-Council supplements its political control of the CRTC, as is exercised by issuing directives to the CRTC under section 27 of the Broadcasting Act.

324 *Id.* at § 23.

List of Representative Readings

R. BABE, CANADIAN TELEVISION BROADCASTING STRUCTURE, PERFORMANCE AND REGULATION (1979)

COMPUTER/COMMUNICATIONS TASK FORCE, BRANCHING OUT: REPORT OF THE COMPUTER/COMMUNICATIONS TASK FORCE (1972).

CONSULTATIVE COMMITTEE ON THE IMPLICATIONS OF TELECOMMUNICATIONS FOR CANADIAN SOVEREIGNTY, DEPARTMENT OF COMMUNICATIONS, TELECOMMUNICATIONS AND CANADA (1979).

DEPARTMENT OF COMMUNICATIONS, INSTANT WORLD: A REPORT ON TELECOMMUNICATIONS IN CANADA (1971).

DEPARTMENT OF COMMUNICATIONS TELECOMMISSION, INTERNATIONAL IMPLICATIONS OF TELECOMMUNICATIONS: THE ROLE OF CANADA IN INTELSAT AND OTHER RELEVANT INTERNATIONAL ORGANIZATIONS (1971).

Donner & Kliman, *The Effect of Section 19.1 of the Income Tax Act on Television Broadcasting*, 32 CAN. TAX J. 1084 (1984).

D. ELLIS, EVOLUTION OF THE CANADIAN BROADCASTING SYSTEM: OBJECTIVES AND REALITIES – 1928-1968 (1979).

ISSUES IN CANADIAN/U.S. TRANSBORDER COMPUTER DATA FLOWS (W. Cundiff & W. Reid eds. 1978).

Juneau, *Audience Fragmentation and Cultural Erosion: A Canadian Perspective on Challenge for the Public Broadcaster*, 35(2) EBU REVIEW 14 (1984).

A. KEYES & C. BRUNET, COPYRIGHT IN CANADA: PROPOSALS FOR A REVISION OF THE LAW (1977).

Mazer, *The Protection of Canadian Culture and the CRTC*, in DECADE OF ADJUSTMENT 97 (J. Menezees ed. 1980).

Montgomery, *The Structure of Telecommunications Regulation and Markets: Canada*, in 4TH WORLD TELECOMMUNICATION FORUM, 1983 (PART III): LEGAL SYMPOSIUM ON INTERNATIONAL INFORMATION NETWORKS III.6.1 (ITU ed. [no date]).

Novotny, *Transborder Data Flow Regulation: Technical Issues of Legal Concern*, 3 COMPUTER L.J. 105 (1982).

F. PEERS, THE PUBLIC EYE: TELEVISION AND THE POLITICS OF CANADIAN BROADCASTING 1952–1968 (1979).

Peers, *Canadian Media Regulation*, in STUDIES IN CANADIAN COMMUNICATIONS 73 (1975).

RESTRICTIVE TRADE PRACTICES COMMISSION, MINISTER OF SUPPLY AND SERVICES, TELECOMMUNICATIONS IN CANADA: PHASE III – THE IMPACT OF VERTICAL INTEGRATION ON THE EQUIPMENT INDUSTRY (1983).

RESTRICTIVE TRADE PRACTICES COMMISSION, MINISTER OF SUPPLY AND SERVICES, TELECOMMUNICATIONS IN CANADA: PHASE I – INTERCONNECTION (1979).

SPECIAL SENATE COMMITTEE ON MASS MEDIA, I REPORT ON MASS MEDIA (1980).

Tarbet, *Use of American Broadcast Signals by Canadian Cable Networks: The CanCom Decision*, 32 BUFFALO L. REV. 731 (1983)

Townsend, *Regulation of Newspaper/Broadcasting, Media Cross-Ownership in Canada*, 33 UNIV. N.B.L.J. 261 (1984).

Yarn, *The Development of Canadian Law on Transborder Data Flow*, 13 GA. J. INT'L & COMP. L. 825 (1983).

NATIONAL REPORT QUESTIONNAIRE*

Part 1: Telephone services

A. Regulation of transborder telephone services

- I. Basic regulations of domestic telecommunications law for transborder telephone services[1]
  - 1. Transformation of international regulations into domestic law and practice
    - a) Survey of the relevant international law
      - aa) Multilateral agreements
      - bb) Bilateral agreements
    - b) Scope of questions of transborder telephone services reserved for national regulation
    - c) Domestic regulatory power to transform international regulations into domestic law and practice
      - aa) Power to issue regulations affecting the domestic sphere[2]
        - aaa) Legislature
        - bbb) Public administration (administrative agencies)
        - ccc) Operating companies (providing telephone services)
      - bb) Power to issue regulations affecting foreign states[2]
        - aaa) Legislature
        - bbb) Administrative agencies
        - ccc) Operating companies
    - d) Contents of the international regulations as transformed into domestic law (including their application and construction)
  - 2. Domestic law unaffected by international law
    - a) Regulatory power[2]
      - aa) Legislature
      - bb) Administrative agencies

* The Questionnaire was prepared by a Work Group at the Max Planck Institute in Hamburg. Under the direction of Prof. E.-J. Mestmäcker, the Group consisted of Thomas Born, Reinhard Ellger, Beate-Katrin Graben and Detlev Witt.

cc) Operating companies

b) Survey of the contents of the domestic law (including application and construction)

II. Legal relations between domestic carriers (networks) providing trans-border telephone services and domestic users of those services

1. Use of telephone services

a) Public networks (common carriers)[3]

aa) Who operates public networks?

bb) Legal requirements for establishment and operation of public networks

aaa) Contents of the requirements

bbb) Power to regulate the requirements, to license operating companies, etc.

ccc) Judicial review or other legal recourse against regulatory decisions

cc) What services may be offered? What services are actually available?

dd) Requirements for access to and conditions for use of public networks[4,5]

aaa) Who has access to the networks?[6]

(1) Ultimate consumers

(2) »Resellers« of transmission services (lessees of network capacity)

(3) Power to regulate access to networks

bbb) Setting of tariffs

(1) Tariff principles

(2) Power to regulate tariffs (or market pricing?)

ccc) Liability (of operating company for malfunction, etc.)

ddd) Technical standards (especially standards for terminal equipment and its usage)

(1) Power to regulate standards (source of regulation: international/national, governmental/private?)

(2) Contents of technical standards

eee) Judicial review or other legal recourse against regulatory decisions

b) Private networks
   aa) Who operates private networks?
   bb) Legal requirements for establishment and operation of private networks[6]
      aaa) Contents of the requirements[7]
      bbb) Regulatory power[7]
      ccc) Judicial review or other legal recourse[7]
   cc) What services may be offered? What services are actually available?
   dd) Are private network operators allowed to sublease networks? If so, under which conditions?
c) Networks operated by closed user groups
   aa) Who operates closed-user-group networks? (e.g., SITA, SWIFT)
   bb) Legal requirements for establishment and operation of closed-user-group networks[6]
      aaa) Contents of requirements[7]
      bbb) Regulatory power[7]
      ccc) Judicial review or other legal recourse[7]
   cc) What services may be offered? What services are actually available?
   dd) Requirements for access to and terms of usage of closed-user-group networks[6,7]
      aaa) Who can become a member of the »user group« and thereby gain access to the network?
      bbb) Setting of tariffs
         (1) Tariff principles
         (2) Who sets the tariffs?
      ccc) Liability (for errors, malfunction, etc.)
      ddd) Technical standards
      eee) Judicial review or other legal recourse; government supervision

2. Admission of terminal equipment to the network[8,9]
   a) What terminal equipment is part of the network – according to domestic telecommunications law – and therefore subject to the regulatory powers governing the telephone services?
   b) Who regulates the admission of terminal equipment to the network?
      aa) Administrative agencies

bb) Network operators
c) Criteria for admission (e.g., technical compatability)[5]
d) Judicial review or other legal recourse

III. Legal relations between domestic and international or foreign network operators

1. Access of domestic networks to and terms of usage of foreign networks
   a) Requirements of domestic telecommunications law[6] for access to the international network[10,11]
      aa) Contents of the requirements
         aaa) International law (multilateral/bilateral agreements) and domestic implementation thereof
         bbb) Domestic law unaffected by international law
      bb) Regulatory power
         aaa) International organizations
         bbb) Bilateral coordination
         ccc) Domestic legislature
         ddd) Domestic administrative agencies
         eee) Operating companies
      cc) Judicial review or other legal recourse
   b) Requirements of domestic telecommunications law for the use of the international network (to what extent does domestic law influence these requirements?)[12]
      aa) Contents of the requirements
         aaa) Setting of tariffs, accounting
            (1) International framework (multilateral/bilateral) agreements, including their transformation into domestic law)
            (2) Domestic law unaffected by international law
         bbb) Technical standards
            (1) International framework
            (2) Domestic law
         ccc) Liability (for malfunction, etc.)
      bb) Regulatory powers for setting tariffs and technical standards
         aaa) International organizations
         bbb) Bilateral coordination
         ccc) Domestic legislature

ddd) Domestic administrative agencies
eee) Operating companies
cc) Judicial review or other legal recourse

2. Access of foreign networks to and terms of usage of domestic networks
   a) Are several domestic networks accessible from abroad?
   b) Requirements of domestic telecommunications law[6] for access to domestic network(s)
      aa) Contents of the requirements
         aaa) International regulations (including their transformation into domestic law)
         bbb) Domestic law unaffected by international law
      bb) Regulatory powers
         aaa) International organizations
         bbb) Bilateral coordination
         ccc) Domestic legislature
         ddd) Domestic administrative agencies
         eee) Operating companies
      cc) Judicial review or other legal recourse
   c) Terms of usage of the national networks
      aa) Contents of the terms
         aaa) Tariffs, accounting between networks
            (1) International framework (including transformation into domestic law)
            (2) Domestic law unaffected by international law
         bbb) Technical standards
            (1) International framework (including transformation into domestic law)
            (2) Domestic law unaffected by international law
         ccc) Liability (for errors, malfunction, etc.)
      bb) Power to regulate tariffs and technical standards
         aaa) International organizations
         bbb) Bilateral coordination
         ccc) Domestic legislature
         ddd) Domestic administrative agencies
         eee) Operating companies
      cc) Judicial review or other legal recourse

B. Legal regulation of the terminal and network equipment markets
  I. Demand side (procurement)
    1. Impact of the regulation of telephone services on the terminal and network equipment market
      a) Who procures the equipment?
        aa) To what extent does the domestic telecommunications law allow the network owners/operators and the users to purchase equipment according to their own choice?
        bb) Competitive situation of network owners/operators in purchasing network and terminal equipment
      b) Conditions of the procurement of equipment
        aa) Power to set the conditions
          aaa) International framework
          bbb) Domestic legislature and administrative agencies
          ccc) Operating companies
        bb) Contents of the conditions
          aaa) Technical standards and research/development of equipment
          bbb) Pricing, contractual terms
          ccc) Who maintains the equipment; under what conditions?
          ddd) Criteria for choice among several suppliers
    2. Impact of further regulations (besides telecommunications law) on the terminal and network equipment markets
      a) Impact of the regulation of foreign trade on the domestic procurement of terminal and network equipment
        aa) General rules for foreign trade in goods
        bb) Particular rules for foreign trade in terminal and network equipment
      b) Impact of other regulations (e.g., antitrust law; general regulation of economic activities)

  II. Supply side
    1. Effect of demand-side situation on the access to the market of network and terminal equipment for suppliers
    2. Impact of economic dependencies and other relations between demand and supply sides on the market for network and terminal equipment

1. This part calls for a survey of the regulations. Details should be given at parts II and III.
2. It should also be described to what extent the relevant institutions have actually exercised their regulatory powers.
3. The notion »public networks« means common carriers that offer their telephone services to all interested parties. The notion includes operators being owners of the networks as well as companies that offer telephone services by means of leased lines.
4. The »users« of public networks may be:
   - customers, who use telephone services for their own needs
   - lessees, who offer telephone services to third parties by means of leased lines
5. In the following parts, the international regulations and their transformation into domestic law should also be considered even if this may not be particularly mentioned in the outline.
6. General regulations other than telecommunications law should also be considered (e.g., antitrust law)
7. As far as private networks are operated by means of lines leased from common carriers, the conditions for access and usage, as stated at Part II.1.a) dd), should be referred to.
8. The different kinds of telephone networks have to be taken into account (see Part II.1.a)–c) above).
9. In this part, regulations regarding terminal equipment should only be dealt with, insofar as the admission of the equipment to the network is concerned. The impact of these regulations on the market for terminal equipment is to be treated in Part B of the outline.
10. The notion »international network« embraces all networks used for transborder telephone services except domestic networks.
11. »Requirements of access« means the criteria for determining which domestic carrier has access to foreign networks.
12. The conditions for access to and usage of networks used for transborder services can only be described comprehensively if the respective foreign telecommunications law is taken into account. This would go beyond the scope of a purely national report. However, information on bilateral relations should be added if available.

Part 2: Remote data processing (also: Videotex and remote sensing)

A. Legal regulation of transborder data processing

I. General legal rules that may be applicable to transborder data processing

1. Export of data
   a) General laws for the protection of national security and public safety (e.g., protection of secrets related to national security)
   b) Rules for the protection of domestic economic interests (e.g., regulations imposing tariffs on exports of data, disquettes, cassettes, hardware and software)
   c) General laws for the protection of private and individual interests
   d) Privacy protection

2) Import of data
   a) General laws for the protection of national security and public safety
   b) Rules for the protection of domestic economic interests (e.g., regulations imposing tariffs on the import of data, disquettes, cassettes, hard- and software)
   c) General laws for the protection of private and individual interests
   d) Privacy protection

II. Regulations relating to transborder data processing as a service

1. Import of data processing services
   a) Commercial data processing services (data processing services offered to third parties that are not members of closed-user-group networks)
      aa) Principles of international business transactions law of the reporting country for transborder business in services in general (especially import regulations)
      bb) Particular rules for data processing services

aaa) Data processing
bbb) Data storage and retrieval

b) Intra-company communication
   aa) Data processing
   bb) Data storage and retrieval
c) Closed-user-group networks
   aa) Data processing
   bb) Data storage and retrieval

2. Export of data processing services
   a) Commercial data processing services (data processing services offered to third parties that are not members of closed-user-group networks)
      aa) Principles of international business transactions law of the reporting country for transborder business in services in general (especially export regulations)
      bb) Particular rules for data processing services
         aaa) Data processing
         bbb) Data storage and retrieval
   b) Intra-company communication
      aa) Data processing
      bb) Data storage and retrieval
   c) Closed-user-group networks
      aa) Data processing
      bb) Data storage and retrieval

III. Regulations applicable specifically to transborder data processing survey of international law

1. Basic legal principles of domestic telecommunications law for the transborder transmission of data[1]
   a) Transformation of legal requirements set up by international law into domestic law and practice
      aa) Survey of the relevant international law
         aaa) Multilateral agreements (e.g., ITU, regional organizations)
         bbb) Bilateral agreements
      bb) Scope of the issues of telecommunications reserved for domestic regulation
      cc) Domestic regulatory power to transform international requirements into domestic law and practice

aaa) Power to issue regulations affecting the domestic sphere and regulations issued[2]
  (1) Legislature
  (2) Administrative agencies
  (3) Operating companies providing data transmission services

bbb) Power to issue regulations affecting the international or foreign sphere
  (1) Legislature
  (2) Administrative agencies
  (3) Operating companies providing data transmission services

dd) Content of the international rules as transformed into domestic law (including application and construction of the rules)

b) Domestic law unaffected by international law
  aa) Regulating Power
    aaa) Legislature
    bbb) Administrative agencies
    ccc) Operating companies
  bb) Survey of the contents of the domestic law (including application and construction)

2. Rules of domestic law regulating the relations between domestic operating companies providing international data transmission services and domestic users of those services
  a) Use of data transmission services
    aa) Public networks (common carriers)[3]
      aaa) Who in fact operates public networks?
      bbb) Legal requirements for installation and operation of public networks
        (1) Content of requirements
        (2) Jurisdiction (for making the regulations and granting licenses, etc.)
        (3) Judicial review or other legal recourse against regulatory decisions
      ccc) What services legally may be offered via the public network?
        (1) Transmission services alone
        (2) Enhanced services (i.e., transmission *and* data

processing services)

ddd) Requirements for access to and use of public networks[4,5]

(1) Jurisdiction to regulate access and use of networks – who actually regulates?

(2) Who has access to the networks?[6]

(2.1) Users (ultimate consumers) of data processing services

(2.2) Offerors of data processing services (who offer data processing services to other parties.

(2.3) Lessees of networks, who offer either transmission services alone or enhanced services

(2) Setting of tariffs

(1.1) Regulatory jurisdiction (or market pricing)

(2.3) Principles of setting tariffs

(3) Liability for errors in data processing

(4) Technical standards (especially for terminal equipment and its usage)

(4.1) Source of regulation: international or national; governmental or private

(4.2) Contents

(5) Judicial review or other legal recourse

bb) Private networks

aaa) Who operates private networks?

bbb) Legal requirements for installation and operation of private networks[6]

(1) Regulatory power[7]

(2) Judicial review or other legal recourse

(3) Contents of requirements[7]

ccc) Which services are offered through private networks?

(1) Data transmission for the network operator only

(2) Data transmission also for third parties

ddd) Are private network operators allowed to sublet the networks? If so, under which conditions is a sublease allowed?

cc) Networks operated by closed user groups[6]

aaa) Who operates closed-user-group networks (e.g., Swift, Sita)?

bbb) Legal requirements for installation and operation of closed-user-group networks[6]

(1) Contents of requirements[7]

(2) Regulatory power[7]

(3) Judicial review and other legal recourse

ccc) What services are offered?

(1) Data transmission for the network operating company only

(2) Data transmission also for third parties

ddd) Conditions for access to and usage of the networks

(1) Who can become a member of the »user group« and thus gain access to the network?

(2) Setting of tariffs

(2.1) Principles

(2.2) Who determines the tariffs?

(3) Liability for errors in data processing

(4) Technical standards

(5) Judicial review or other legal recourse

(6) Government supervision of private networks

b) Admission of terminal equipment[8,9]

aa) Who regulates the admission of terminal equipment to the network?

aaa) Public authorities

bbb) Operating companies

bb) What terminal equipment is part of the network according to domestic telecommunications law and is therefore subject to the respective regulatory powers?

cc) Criteria for admission (e.g., technical standards for compatibility; non-discriminatory competition for foreign suppliers of terminal equipment)

dd) Judicial review or other legal recourse

3. Rules regulating the relations between domestic and international or foreign network operators

a) Access to and modes of usage of international networks[10,11] by domestic carriers

aa) Requirements of domestic telecommunications law for access to international networks[12]

aaa) Contents of requirements
- (1) International preconditions (multilateral or bilateral agreements)
- (2) domestic telecommunications law

bbb) Regulatory powers
- (1) International organizations
- (2) Bilateral agreements
- (3) Domestic legislation
- (4) Domestic administrative agencies
- (5) Operating companies

bb) Requirements of domestic telecommunications law for the use of international networks (to what extent are these conditions influenced by domestic law?)[14]

aaa) Contents of conditions
- (1) Tariffs, accounting
  - (1.1) The international framework (bilateral and multilateral agreements and their transformation into domestic rules)
  - (1.2) Domestic law unaffected by international law
- (2) Technical standards
  - (2.1) International framework
  - (2.2) Domestic Law
- (3) Liability for errors in data transmission

bbb) Regulatory powers for setting tariffs and technical standards
- (1) International institutions
- (2) Bilateral agreements
- (3) Domestic legislation
- (4) Domestic administrative agencies
- (5) Operating companies

ccc) Judicial review and other legal recourse

b) Access to and modes of usage of domestic networks by foreign network operators

aa) How many domestic networks are accessible from abroad?

bb) Requirements set by domestic telecommunications law[6] for access to domestic networks

aaa) Contents of requirements
- (1) International framework

(2) Domestic law

bbb) Regulatory powers

(1) International organizations

(2) Bilateral agreements

(3) Domestic legislation

(4) Domestic administrative agencies

(5) Operating companies

ccc) Judicial review or other legal recourse

cc) Conditions for the use of domestic networks

aaa) Contents of conditions

(1) Tariffs, accounting between domestic and international networks

(1.1) International framework and transformation into domestic law

(1.2) Domestic law

(2) Technical standards

(2.1) International framework and transformation into domestic law

(2.2) Domestic law

(3) Liability for errors in data transmission

bbb) Regulatory powers over tariffs and technical standards

(1) International institutions

(2) Bilateral agreements

(3) Domestic legislation

(4) Domestic administrative agencies

(5) Operating companies

ccc) Judicial review or other legal recourse

B. Regulation of the markets for network and terminal equipment

I. Demand side

1. Impacts of the regulation of data transmission services on the markets for network and terminal equipment

a) Demand

aa) To what extent does the domestic telecommunications law allow the operating companies or the users to purchase network and terminal equipment according to their own choice?

bb) Competition among the network operators in purchasing network and terminal equipment

b) Conditions of procurement of network and terminal equipment

aa) Regulatory powers to set conditions

aaa) International framework

bbb) Domestic legislature and administrative agencies

ccc) Conditions set by operating companies themselves

bb) Contents of the conditions

aaa) Technical standards and development of equipment

bbb) Pricing, contractual conditions

ccc) Maintenance of equipment; conditions

ddd) Criteria for choice among several suppliers

2. Impact of other regulations (besides the rules for data transmission services) on the market for network and terminal equipment

a) Effects of the rules regulating international business transactions upon the market for network and terminal equipment

aa) General provisions for the trade in goods

bb) Particular rules for network and terminal equipment within the law relating to international business transactions

b) Impact of other regulations, e.g., antitrust law, especially regulations against misuse of demand power; general regulation of economic activities

II. Supply side

1. Effect of the demand-side situation on access to the market for network and terminal equipment

2. Impacts of economic dependencies and other relations between the supply and demand sides on competition in the market for network and terminal equipment

1. This part of the outline calls for a survey of the regulations. Details should be given at parts III 2 and 3.
2. The constitutional framework of the legislative activities as well as the content of the provisions should be explained.
3. »Public networks« means common carriers, which offer their data transmission services to any interested parties. »Operating companies« includes the owners of the networks and also companies that use leased lines to offer data transmission services.
4. »Users« of public networks may be:
   - customers, who use the data transmission services for the remote processing for their own needs
   - lessees, who use leased lines to offer third parties remote data processing capacities.
5. Also the international regulations and their transformation into domestic law are to be considered, even if this may not be particularly mentioned in the outline.
6. Also legal rules other than telecommunications law should be taken into account here (e.g., antitrust law)
7. If the private networks are operated with lines leased from common carriers, the conditions for access and usage of the networks are to be treated, as stated at part III 2a, aa, ddd, dd above.
8. At this point, the different kinds of data transmission methods have to be taken into account (see part III 2a above)
9. Regulations relating to terminal equipment should be dealt with here only insofar as the admission of the equipment to the network is concerned. The impact of these regulations on the market for terminal equipment is to be treated in part B of the outline
10. Account should be taken of whether the regulation of access to international networks distinguishes
    a) between different kinds of data to be transmitted or different kinds of data transmission services
    b) between »pure« data transmission services and enhanced services.
11. If special rules exist for the transit of data on the way to third countries, they should be mentioned separately.
12. The notion of »international networks« encompasses all networks that are used for transborder data transmissions, except domestic networks.
13. »Requirements of access« means the criteria for determining which

domestic carrier has access to foreign networks.

14. The conditions under which networks for transborder data transmissions may be accessed and used can only be covered comprehensively if the respective foreign telecommunications law is taken into account. Although this goes beyond the scope of a national report, information on bilateral relations should be added if available.

Part 3: Audiovisual media programmes

A. Regulation of the flow of media programmes from abroad to the reporting state (RS)
(Admission of programmes to the domestic territory; principles and conditions of access)

I. Legal relations between foreign states and programme and transmitting companies on the one hand and the reporting state on the other

1. The international framework and its transformation into national law
(Extent of international obligations of RS to give access to its territory for foreign programmes)
a) Multilateral agreements and international organizations subscribed to by RS
aa) ITU convention and rules arising from it
aaa) Relation of RS to ITU
bbb) Audiovisual broadcast programmes
(1) Jamming
(2) Prohibition of reception
(3) Technical standards and import regulations for receiver equipment
(4) Different treatment according to origin and/or domicile of foreign programme/transmitting company
ccc) Direct-Broadcast Satellites (DBS)
(1) Jamming
(2) Prohibition of reception
(3) Technical standards and import regulations for receiver equipment
(4) Different treatment according to origin and/or domicile of foreign programme/ transmitter company
(5) Different treatment of intended/unintended overspill
ddd) Cable TV (CATV)
(1) Ability of foreign cable operators to link their

systems with domestic cable networks

(1.1) General conditions of access

(1.2) Setting of tariffs

(1.3) Technical standards

(1.4) Programme standards

(2) Access to networks for foreign programmes

(1.1) General conditions of access

(1.2) Setting of tariffs

(1.3) Technical standards

(1.4) Programme standards

bb) Transformation of ITU rules into national law (for broadcast, DBS and CATV programmes)

aaa) Power to transform ITU rules into national law

bbb) Form and extent of transformation

ccc) Jurisdiction for application of transformed rules to foreign programmes of companies

ddd) Practice of application

eee) Judicial review or other legal recourse against regulatory decisions

cc) Human Rights Conventions and rules arising from them

aaa) Extent of adoption by RS

bbb) Audiovisual broadcast programmes

(1) Jamming

(2) Prohibition of reception

(3) Technical standards and import regulations for receiver equipment

(4) Preferential treatment of states of programme companies

ccc) Direct-Broadcast Satellites

– subdivided as above bbb)

ddd) Cable television

– subdivided as above bbb)

dd) Transformation of Human Rights Convention into national law (for broadcast, DBS and CATV)

aaa) Power for transformation of Human Rights Conventions into international law

bbb) Form and extent of transformation

ccc) Jurisdiction for application of transformed

rules to foreign programmes of companies
ddd) Practice of application
eee) Judical review or other legal recourse against regulatory decisions
ee) Other multilateral agreements subscribed to by RS
aaa) Audiovisual broadcast programmes
bbb) Direct-Broadcast Satellites
ccc) Cable Television (CATV)
ff) Transformation of other multilateral agreements into national law (broadcast, DBS and CATV)
– subdivided as above dd) –
b) Bilateral agreements
aaa) Scope left for bilateral agreements under ITU rules
(1) Audiovisual broadcast programmes
(2) Direct-Broadcast Satellites
(3) Cable television (CATV)
bbb) Noteworthy bilateral agreements to which RS subscribes
ccc) Special rules provided by bilateral agreements to which RS subscribes
(1) Audiovisual broadcast programmes
(1.1) Jamming
(1.2) Technical standards and import regulations for receiver equipment
(1.3) Preferential treatment for certain states/programme companies
(1.4) Bilateral monopolies
(2) Direct-Broadcast Satellites
– subdivided as above (1)
(3) Cable television
– subdivided as above (1)
c) Summary: Scope of action left to reporting state under international law or international law as transformed into national law for regulation of access of audiovisual broadcast programmes to its territory.

2. National law independent of international framework (Regulations generally governing the emission of audiovisual broadcast, satellite and cable programmes)
a) Structure of the domestic media and their regulation

aa) Constitutional bases of the national media organization
    aaa) Newspapers, magazines and other print media
    bbb) Audiovisual broadcast programmes
    ccc) Direct-Broadcast Satellites
    ddd) Cable television
bb) Power to regulate, legal technique or regulation
    – subdivided as above aa)
cc) Essentials of the national media regulation
    – subdivided as above aa)

b) General laws applicable to media programmes (classified according to legal spheres or objects of legal protection, e.g.:
   - General laws
   - Penal laws
   - Law against obscenity
   - Law of advertising
   - Antitrust law
   - Other telecommunications laws)

c) Specific applicability of national law, actually or potentially, to incoming foreign programmes
   aa) Audiovisual broadcast programmes
   bb) Direct-Broadcast Satellites
   cc) Cable television

II. Legal relations between reporting state and receivers (Regulations governing the *reception* of broadcast/cable transmitted programmes and legal recourse of receivers to enforce rights of reception)

1. The international framework and its transformation into national law
   a) Multilateral agreements
      aa) ITU convention and rules arising from it
         aaa) Audiovisual broadcast programmes
            (1) Prohibition of reception
            (2) Technical standards and import/operating regulations for receiver equipment
            (3) Tariffs for reception
         bbb) Direct-Broadcast Satellites
            – subdivided as above aaa)

ccc) Cable television
  (1) Principles of access to networks
  (2) Technical standards and import/operating regulations for receiver equipment
  (3) Tariffs for access
bb) Human rights convention and rules arising from them
 aaa) Audiovisual broadcast programmes
  (1) Prohibition of reception
  (2) Technical standards and import regulations for receiver equipment
  (3) Tariffs for reception
 bbb) Direct-Broadcast Satellites
  – subdivided as above aaa)
 ccc) Cable television
  – subdivided as above aaa)

b) Bilateral agreements
 aa) Frame for bilateral agreements under multilateral rules
  aaa) Audiovisual broadcast programmes
  bbb) Direct-Broadcast Satellites
  ccc) Cable television
 bb) Rules provided by bilateral programmes
  aaa) Audiovisual broadcast programmes
   (1) Technical standards and import regulations for receiver equipment
   (2) Tariffs
  bbb) Direct-Broadcast Satellites
   – subdivided as above aaa)
  ccc) Cable television
   – subdivided as above aaa)

c) Transformation of international agreements on receiver's rights into national law (for broadcast, DBS and CATV programmes)
 aa) Power for transformation of rules into national law
 bb) Form and content of transformation
 cc) Jurisdiction for application of transformed rules
 dd) Practice of application
 ee) Judicial review or other legal recourse against regulatory decisions

d) Summary: Scope of action left to reporting state under international law for regulation of relations between state and receivers of broadcast/cable-transmitted programmes from abroad

2. National law independent of international framework (Regulations governing the *reception* of broadcast/cable transmitted programmes for reasons of public interest)
   a) Constitutional framework of audivisual media reception (Civil rights of receivers and their judicial review)
      aa) Audiovisual broadcast programmes
      bb) Direct-Broadcast Satellites
      cc) Cable television
   b) Power to regulate, legal technique of regulation
      – subdivided as above a)
   c) Content of regulations (Audiovisual broadcast, DBS and CATV)
      aa) Prohibition of reception/principles of access to networks
      bb) Technical standards, manufacturing and operating interdictions for receiver equipment
      cc) Reception tariffs

III. Legal relations between media companies and individuals, including personal claims against companies (Audiovisual broadcast, DBS and CATV)

1. International agreements and their transformation into national law
   a) Protection of privacy law; protection of honour; right to have a counter-statement published
   b) Copyright law
   c) Illicit advertising (individual claims)

2. Conflict law of the reporting state
   – subdivided as above 1.

3. National rules providing individual claims against programme companies and thus potential barriers to free transborder flow of media programmes
   – subdivided as above 1.

B. Establishment and activities of foreign programme companies/programme transmitting companies *on the territory of the RS*

I. International framework

1. Establishment and operation of transmitter stations and cable networks
   a) Audiovisual broadcast programmes
   b) Direct-Broadcast Satellites (including participation in national satellite operating companies, operations of national satellite systems)
   c) Cable television (establishment and operation of cable networks)

2. Establishment and activities of programme companies
   a) Multilateral agreements (e.g., EEC-treaty)
      aaa) Audiovisual broadcast programmes
      bbb) Direct-Broadcast Satellites
      ccc) Cable television
   b) Bilateral agreements (e.g., AFN, RFE)
      – subdivided as above a)

II. National framework
   – subdivided as above I.

C. Regulation of the flow of media programmes transmitted from reporting state to other countries (legal relations between RS and programme companies transmitting to other countries)

I. International framework and its transformation into national law

1. ITU convention and rules arising from it
   a) Audiovisual broadcast programmes
      (rights of RS to transmit abroad)
   b) Direct-Broadcast Satellites
      (Orbital positions of RS)
   c) Cable television
      Access of domestic programmes to foreign cable systems)

2. Other multilateral agreements
   – subdivided as above 1.

3. Bilateral agreements
   – subdivided as above 1.

II. National law independent of international framework

1. Regulations governing the establishment and operation of transmitting facilities
   a) Constitutional framework
      aa) Audiovisual broadcast programmes
      bb) Direct-Broadcast Satellites
      cc) Cable networks
   b) Power to regulate, legal technique of regulation
      – subdivided as above a)
   c) Content of regulations
      aa) Principles of authorization
         aaa) Audiovisual broadcast programmes
         bbb) Direct-Broadcast Satellites
         ccc) Cable television
      bb) Rules governing the content of programmes
         – subdivided as above aa)
      cc) Other conditions of authorization, including tariffs
         – subdivided as above aa)

2. Regulations governing the production of programmes for abroad
   – subdivided as above 1.

Ernst-Joachim Mestmäcker (ed.),

Law and Economics of Transborder Telecommunications – Symposium.

Die Beiträge zu diesem Symposium behandeln das Zusammenspiel zwischen nationalen und internationalen Telekommunikationssystemen. An der Konferenz, die vom 2. bis 6.3.1986 in Malente stattfand, haben die an dem Institutsprojekt beteiligten Wissenschaftler, insbesondere die Autoren der Länderberichte, Beamte der zuständigen Behörden und Vertreter der Wirtschaft teilgenommen. Die Länderberichte, die in dieser Reihe gesondert veröffentlicht werden, ermöglichen den Vergleich verschiedener nationaler Erfahrungen, zeigen deren Bedeutung für die grenzüberschreitende Telekommunikation und enthalten Hinweise auf bereits entstandene und potentielle internationale Konflikte. In der Entscheidung über nationale Politiken für den Export und den Import von Informationen müssen die Staaten den Zusammenhang mit dem internationalen Kommunikationssystem in Rechnung stellen. Die Mehrheit der Beiträge behandelt die daraus entstehenden Zusammenhänge nationaler und internationaler Regulierungen, Harmonisierungen und Kooperationen.

1987, 450 S., 139,– DM, Subskr.-Preis 119,– DM (Bd. 1), ISBN 3-7890-1368-4

Arbeitskreis Werbefernsehen der deutschen Wirtschaft,
Redaktion Wolfgang Hainer

Europafernsehen und Werbung

Chancen für die deutsche und europäische Medienpolitik - Fachtagung am 24. und 25. September 1986 in Haus Rissen/Hamburg

---

Wie wird europäisches Fernsehen aussehen? Welche Auswirkungen hat die Arbeit der Europäischen Kommission auf nationale Rundfunkordnungen? Welche Rolle fällt ihr bei der Werbung zu? Auf der Basis des Entwurfs der EG-Direktive zum Rundfunkrecht veranstaltete der Arbeitskreis Werbefernsehen der deutschen Wirtschaft Ende September 1986 in Hamburg eine Tagung, die durch Referate kompetenter Referenten aus zahlreichen Bereichen diese Fragen beleuchtete. Besondere Bedeutung auch in der anschließenden Diskussion unter der Moderation von Hartmut Froels nahm das von Prof. Dr. Friauf vorgelegte Gutachten ein, wonach der Schutz der Meinungsfreiheit nach Art. 10 Europäische Menschenrechtskonvention und Art. 5 Grundgesetz auch für die Werbung gilt. Die Staatssekretäre Schleyer und Leister stellten Folgerungen für die nationale Medienpolitik dar; der Präsident des Bundeskartellamts beleuchtete das Wettbewerbsverhältnis zwischen privaten und öffentlich-rechtlichen Programmveranstaltern, die in ihren Äußerungen verschiedene Akzente für Notwendigkeit einer Weiterentwicklung des Rundfunkmarktes setzten. Neues Zahlenmaterial zum Europafernsehen legte der Vorsitzende des AKW vor. Die mit großer Sachkenntnis und Intensität geführten Diskussionen sind in dem Band zusammengefaßt wiedergegeben.

1987, 148 S., Salesta brosch., 39,– DM ISBN 3-7890-1362-5